NUMBER POWER

A Cooperative Approach to Mathematics and Social Development

Grade 2, Volume 2: Informal Computation and Number Relationships

Julie Wellington Contestable

Carol Tensing Westrich

Shaila Regan

Susie Alldredge

Laurel Robertson

DEVELOPMENTAL STUDIES CENTER

2000 Embarcadero, Suite 305

Oakland, CA 94606

This material is based upon work supported by the National Science Foundation under Grant No. ESI-9150104.

Any opinions, findings, and conclusions, or recommendations expressed in this material are those of the author(s) and do not necessarily reflect the views of the National Science Foundation.

Number Power™ was developed by the Cooperative Mathematics Project, a program of the Developmental Studies Center, 2000 Embarcadero, Suite 305, Oakland, California 94606.

Design: Don Taka
Illustrations: Duane Bibby
Cover Design: John Sullivan/Visual Stategies

ISBN 1-57621-199-1

Contents

Unit 1
Number Meaning and Relationships

Unit 2
Mental and Informal Computation

Unit 3
Informal Computation

Acknowledgments

Many people were involved in the development and production of *Number Power™*. We are grateful for their time, valuable suggestions, and encouragement.

We wish to express our deep appreciation to the National Science Foundation, and in particular Margaret Cozzens and Eric Robinson, for their support of our program.

We also wish to thank the members of our Advisory Board, who contributed enormously to the development of the *Number Power* program:

Joan Akers, California Department of Education
Carne Barnett, WestEd, San Francisco, California
Neil Davidson, University of Maryland
Carol Langbort, San Francisco State University
Nel Noddings, Stanford University
Ruth Parker, Collaborative Learning Associates, Ferndale, Washington
Paul Trafton, University of Northern Iowa
Jean Stenmark, EQUALS, Lawrence Hall of Science, University of California, Berkeley
Julian Weissglass, University of California, Santa Barbara

Many teachers piloted lessons and units, allowed us in their classrooms to teach or to observe, and provided us with feedback that helped shape the format and content of the program. We particularly wish to acknowledge the following teachers and math specialists:

California

Alameda City Unified School District
Jane Baldi

Albany City Unified School District
Nancy Bowen
Barbara Brunetti
Nancy Johnson
Violet Nicholas
Greta Olsen
Susie Ronfeldt
Victoria Sears
Sharon Trott

Burlingame Unified School District
Nancy Butte
Becky Glover
Nancy Kaye
Amy Sanford

Berkeley Unified School District
Carolyn Adams
Mary Ough

Mount Diablo School District
Denise Cebalo
Mez Chafe-Powles
Donna D'Amico
Nancy Geralski
Glenn Lucey
Nancy Yee

Moraga Elementary School District
Dawn Jakobsen
Ruth Manlove

Moreland Elementary School District
Terry Baker
Wanda Binford
Pat Brigham
Cristine Bryant
Carolyn Cassell
Shari Clare
Jan Frosberg
Vivian Karpel
Lew Osborn
Terry Pomposo
Linda Stumpf
Gaby Tennant

Oakland Unified School District
Mike Butzen
Gloria Durflinger
Roz Haberkern
Alicia Rivera
Kathy Selleck
Ted Sugarman
Sue Tierney
Lisa Wong

Pittsburg Unified School District
Lisa Abono

Redwood City Elementary School District
Kris Dalrymple
Lisa Erskine
Frances Nuss
Ann Marie Sulzbach

Ross Elementary School District
Allison Quoyeser

John Swett Unified School District
Kay Balandra
Louise Bevilaqua
Marilyn Griego
Erin Hallisy
Sandra Krey
Anita Pister
Jackie Schlemmer
Cathy Shipp
Carol Westrich

San Ramon Valley Unified School District
Michele Brynjulson
Cindy Collins
Carolyn Costamagna
Cheryl Gonzales
Deneka Horaleck
Louise Lotz
Lincoln Olbrycht
Sally Powers
Sue Smith
Ruby Tellsworth

Stockton City Unified School District
Jan Holloway

Vallejo City Unified School District
Howard Banford

Illinois

St. Charles School District
Maggie Haroldson

Canada

School District No. 39, Vancouver, British Columbia
Shirley Brunke
Pat Craig
Joan Crockett
Wayne Gatley
Liz Gautschi
Linda O'Reilly
Jan Renouf
Carrie Sleep

We wish to thank the following past and present staff of, and consultants to, the Developmental Studies Center for their support and invaluable contributions to the *Number Power* series:

Eric Schaps, President
Judy Kingsley, Managing Director
Pam Herrera, Director of Administration
Victor Battistich, Deputy Director of Research
Carol Berger, Administrative Assistant
Duane Bibby, Illustrator
Allan Ferguson, Art Director
Susan Frost, Production Editor
Anne Goddard, Editor
Leigh McLellan, Desktop Publisher
John Prestianni, Desktop Publisher
Jared Simpson, Editor

About the Authors

Julie Wellington Contestable
Curriculum Developer

Ms. Contestable has more than fifteen years of experience as an elementary classroom teacher, mentor for language arts and mathematics, and mathematics specialist. She has been a leader in district and county mathematics committees and in California School Improvement Program reviews. She is a past officer of the Alameda/Contra Costa Counties Mathematics Educators.

Carol Tensing Westrich
Curriculum Developer

Ms. Westrich has extensive experience at the elementary level, both as a classroom teacher and more recently as a reading specialist. She has been a master teacher and a leader and staff developer for the California School Improvement Program. As a district mentor, Ms. Westrich developed curriculum that integrated mathematics and language arts. She also holds an advanced degree in Reading Leadership.

Shaila Regan
Codirector/ Curriculum Developer

Ms. Regan has extensive experience as an elementary school mathematics specialist and classroom teacher. She has also been a mathematics consultant and staff developer for public and private schools throughout the United States, and is past president of the Alameda/Contra Costa Counties Mathematics Educators.

Susie Alldredge
Curriculum Developer

Ms. Alldredge received an M.A. in Education in Math, Science, and Technology from the University of California, Berkeley, where her research focused on instructional methods to enhance students' number sense. She has been a master teacher for the U.C. Berkeley teacher training program, and she received an award for outstanding mathematics teaching from the Alameda/Contra Costa Counties Mathematics Educators.

Laurel Robertson
Director

Dr. Robertson has been in education for more than twenty-five years as a classroom teacher, staff developer, mathematics consultant, and director of several educational programs. She is past president of the California Association for Cooperation in Education and has been a member of the board of directors of the International Association for the Study of Cooperation in Education.

Preface

This is an exciting time to be a mathematics teacher. Educators and the general public alike are calling for fundamental changes in the content and process of mathematics instruction. Recent national reports document the need for change, describe new goals for the field, and suggest new approaches to teaching and learning.

Number Power™ is designed to meet the call for curricula that model new instructional strategies and content. The focus of the program is to support and expand students' emerging number sense. The *Number Power* program consists of three multiweek units each for kindergarten, first, fourth, fifth, and sixth grades, and six multiweek units each for second and third grades. The program is intended to supplement or replace existing curricula aimed at developing number concepts.

The *Number Power* units provide opportunities for all students to construct and expand their understanding of number as they engage in and reflect on experiences that help them make mathematical connections, employ mathematical tools, work with others to solve problems, and communicate about their thinking. The units are designed to be accessible to all students and to meet the needs of students with diverse backgrounds and experiences. Each unit fosters the development of several essential concepts and may include other areas of mathematics, such as measurement, geometry, and data analysis.

Number Power takes a holistic, developmental view of education and is designed to enhance students' social, as well as mathematical, development. Cooperative group work and ongoing discussion about group interaction help students understand the need to be fair, caring, and responsible, and develop the skills needed to work successfully with others.

Focus and Use of Grade 2, Volume 2: *Informal Computation and Number Relationships*

The units in this volume are designed to help students build their understanding of the relationship between two- and three-digit numbers and to develop strategies to carry out mental and informal computations. In Unit 1, students explore the number 100 and extend their understanding to numbers greater than 100. In Unit 2, students build mental computation strategies as they play games with dice, spinners, and various game boards such as the 1–120 chart. In Unit 3, students develop, use, and explain strategies as they solve addition and subtraction problems that arise from data they collect about their names.

The units in Volume 2 are intended to be taught in order. They are designed for students with some prior experience exploring place value concepts and grouping and counting by ones, tens, and hundreds. If students have not had these experiences, you may wish to first teach the units in Grade 2, Volume 1: *Grouping, Place Value, and Informal Computation.*

The social development in this volume complements and extends the social development in Volume 1. Students continue to develop group skills, share the work, reach agreement, and make decisions. They think about how to treat each other considerately as they play games and solve problems with a partner. They take responsibility for their learning in pair work and think about what it means to use materials such as calculators, dice, and beans in a responsible way. Throughout the three units students have opportunities to reflect on how their behavior affects others and the group work.

Number Sense and Social Development

Number Power is based on the assumption that children learn about the world through everyday interaction with their environment and with others. Academic and social learning are integrated naturally, rather than developed in isolation from each other. Exploration, questioning, discussion, and reasoning are all part of this natural learning process.

With this in mind, *Number Power* has been designed to support children's mathematical and social development in an integrated manner by actively engaging them in exploration and reasoning with others. Students in pairs and/or as a class investigate open-ended questions; use a wide variety of tools; develop problem-solving strategies; collect, organize, and analyze data; and record and communicate their thinking and results. Children's sense of number is fostered; their understanding of what it means to be fair, caring, and responsible is developed; and their ability to act on these values is enhanced.

Number Sense

The mathematical focus of *Number Power* is to develop children's number sense. A sound understanding of number is indispensable to making sense of the world. Documents such as *Reshaping School Mathematics* (Mathematical Sciences Education Board, 1990), *Curriculum and Evaluation Standards for School Mathematics* (National Council of Teachers of Mathematics, 1989), and the *NCTM: Standards 2000* (National Council of Teachers of Mathematics, projected publication date, Spring 2000) make it clear that the development of students' number sense should be a primary goal of elementary school mathematics programs.

Children come to school with some understanding of the meaning of numbers, of how numbers relate to each other, and of how numbers can be used to describe quantities. *Number Power* builds on and extends this conceptual understanding by providing opportunities for students to explore and use numbers as they solve problems, discuss their thinking about numbers, and make connections between their experience and underlying concepts.

Number Power uses a combination of hands-on experiences and reflection on these experiences to enhance children's sense of number meaning,

number relationships, and the relative magnitude of numbers. Students begin to think flexibly about numbers and to understand, for example, that 24 is 2 twelves, 20 plus 4, almost 25, about half of 50, small compared to 100, and large compared to 3. Children also begin to develop "benchmarks"—recognizing, for example, that 70 is closer to 50 than to 100.

Number Power strives to deepen children's understanding of how operations affect numbers. They have many opportunities to informally use addition, subtraction, multiplication, and division to solve problems and to develop their own algorithms for these operations. Students begin to develop a sense of the effect of using a number as an operator on other numbers—understanding, for example, what happens when a number is increased by ten or decreased by ten. Students have many opportunities to construct an understanding of the relationships among operations.

Number Power involves students in experiences that help them explore referents for numbers, make and use estimates, and begin to develop a range of possible quantities for a given situation. These experiences help students begin to relate an understanding of number to real-world situations. They begin to recognize, for example, that a dog would not weigh 800 pounds or that it is reasonable that a new car would cost $15,000.

Within a variety of problem-solving and real-life contexts, such as playing games with dice, collecting objects, and collecting and analyzing data about their names, children are encouraged to

- think of number as quantity;
- make sense of numbers and judge the reasonableness of solutions;
- have conversations about numbers;
- visualize number patterns;
- use a variety of computational methods: manipulatives, pencil and paper, mental computation, and calculator; and
- make estimates.

As they explore numbers, children devise and use problem-solving strategies and discuss their methods with others. Through such direct, personal experiences, students continue to construct their understanding of number and to enhance their ability to make sense of the world of mathematics.

Social Development

Traditionally, schools have taken a major role in the socialization of students, helping them to become responsible citizens. In recent decades, this role has taken a backseat to academic preparation, as students and schools have been judged almost entirely by their success in meeting narrow academic standards.

Today, however, the stresses of our rapidly changing world require schools to refocus attention on students' social development while continuing to support their academic development. In order to prepare students for future challenges, schools must help them

- be creative, thoughtful, and knowledgeable;
- develop a lifelong love of learning and the ability to pursue their own learning goals;
- be principled, responsible, and humane; and
- be able to work effectively with others to solve problems.

The recognition that social development and academic learning are integral to schooling and occur simultaneously is a cornerstone of *Number Power*. In each lesson, students have opportunities to explore and solve problems with others and to discuss and reflect on their group interaction. In the process, students are encouraged to balance their own needs with the needs of others, to recognize how their behavior affects others, to think about the underlying values that guide behavior, and to develop appropriate group skills. Reflection on their experience helps students construct their understanding of social and cultural norms and leads to a deeper integration of positive social values in their lives.

Using Cooperative Group Work in Your Classroom

Cooperative group work benefits all students, both academically and socially. When students with different abilities, backgrounds, and perspectives explain and demonstrate their thinking and listen to the thinking of others, their reasoning and communication skills are fostered. Additionally, they are exposed to new ideas and strategies, learn to be supportive of and to value others, and become more positive about themselves as learners and more motivated to learn.

What Is the *Number Power* Approach?

The *Number Power* approach to cooperative group work includes some elements common to most cooperative learning methods: students work in heterogeneous pairs or groups to pursue a common goal; are actively involved in their learning; and have ongoing opportunities to share ideas, discuss their thinking, and hear the thinking of others.

The *Number Power* approach differs from other cooperative learning methods in several respects, but particularly in its focus on social development. Beyond addressing group skills, *Number Power* places emphasis on encouraging students to be responsible for their own learning and behavior and on helping students construct their understanding of

- what it means to be fair, caring, and responsible;
- why these values are important; and
- how these values can be acted on as students interact with others.

Another difference is that the *Number Power* approach does not specify role assignments for group work. Instead, the lessons provide opportunities for students to decide such things as how they will divide the work and how they will record and report their findings. Learning how to make these decisions helps students become responsible group members. Many of the lessons include examples of questions that help students think about how they made these decisions and what they learned that would help them the next time they work together.

The *Number Power* approach recognizes that a strong mathematics program includes a variety of instructional methods. The program, therefore, includes some direct instruction and individual work. However, *Number Power* lessons are structured to provide frequent opportunities for students to interact with each other and with the teacher. Cooperative work and class discussion alternate throughout the lessons. Many lessons begin with a class discussion about a problem or question, sometimes relating to a previous exploration. During group work, students are asked open-ended questions to extend their thinking, to help them solve mathematical and social problems, and to informally assess their conceptual development. At times, the class meets to discuss strategies and solutions and to raise new questions to explore. Lessons conclude with an opportunity for groups and the class to reflect on their mathematical work and social interaction.

The *Number Power* approach views assessment as an integral part of instruction. To help you assess students' conceptual and social development and make further instructional decisions, the lessons suggest opportune times to observe individuals and groups and suggest questions to ask yourself and students. Each lesson provides opportunities for you to learn more about your students' development as they explain their thinking verbally, in writing, through drawings, and by demonstration. Open-ended investigations allow students with different levels of conceptual understanding to approach problems in their own ways and allow you to assess the strategies students bring to the experience and how their conceptual understanding develops over time. The open-endedness of these experiences also allows you to assess students' flexibility, perseverance, and ability to discover multiple solutions and strategies.

Throughout the *Number Power* lessons, asking probing, open-ended questions is of paramount importance in helping students construct their understanding. The questions suggested in the lessons may often be answered in more than one way and elicit a variety of strategies from students. Whether problems have multiple solutions or one right answer, the questions are designed to help students examine, verify, and compare different strategies and to help them rely on reasoning and number sense to solve problems. At first, young children may have difficulty explaining their thinking, but their ability to express themselves increases with practice and with the opportunity to hear the explanations of other children.

Many of the *Number Power* lessons suggest the use of some easily implemented cooperative learning strategies that provide opportunities for students to share their thinking. (For more information about cooperative strategies, see *Blueprints for a Cooperative Classroom,* by the Developmental Studies Center, or Spencer Kagan's *Cooperative Learning.* See Additional Reading, p. 167.)

1. *Turn to Your Partner.* Students turn to a person sitting next to them to discuss an issue or question.

2. *Think, Pair, Share.* Students individually take a short period of time to think about a question or issue and then discuss their thoughts with a partner. Pairs report their thinking to another pair or to the class. This strategy is especially appropriate when students are asked to respond to complex questions and those requiring mental computation

3. *Tea Party.* Pairs circulate around the classroom. When you call, "Tea Party," pairs stop moving, turn to the nearest pair, and share information on a suggested topic. Pairs are then asked to

move around the room again for as many "Tea Parties" as seem appropriate for the topic and for students' interest. "Tea Party" discussion topics might include sharing ideas about numbers, comparing and discussing quantities, and finding and discussing number combinations. To introduce and practice this strategy, students might discuss topics such as favorite colors, favorite numbers, favorite breakfast foods, their pets, and their birthdays.

4. *Strolling.* Students display their work on their desks or tables and then stroll around the room to view the work of others. Students can stroll individually, in pairs, or in groups. They can talk about what they see as they stroll or after they stroll. Students might stroll to view such things as pattern block designs made by individuals, pairs, or groups; graphs; items brought for sharing; artwork; and favorite books.

5. *Stroll and Stop.* This is a strategy similar to "Strolling," except that students stop on a signal from the teacher and spend some time viewing the work of others.

6. *Think, Pair, Write.* Like "Think, Pair, Share," students have an opportunity to think individually before discussing their thoughts with a partner. Pairs then write about their thinking. They might share their writing with another pair, with the class, or with you.

7. *Heads Together.* Students in groups of four put their heads together to discuss an issue or question among themselves.

8. *Group Brainstorming.* This strategy requires that each group select someone to record ideas. After groups list as many ideas as they can about a topic or a problem, they are given time to organize or sort them.

How Do I Begin?

Even if you have used cooperative learning strategies before, it is a good idea to start slowly. Begin with pairs rather than larger group sizes and try the cooperative learning strategies suggested in the previous section. These and other strategies can be adapted to the teaching of any subject and can be used to structure student interaction before, during, and after traditional or cooperative lessons.

An important factor in helping students become responsible, independent, and cooperative learners is the establishment of an environment that supports cooperation. Such an environment makes students feel safe, assures them that their efforts and opinions are valued and respected, and provides them with many opportunities to make choices and decisions. The role you play and the behavior you model are crucial to the development of this environment. For example, asking questions that help students solve a problem on their own encourages them to become responsible for their learning and shows that you value their ability to do so. Asking open-ended questions beginning with such words as *what*, *why*, and *how* helps students extend their understanding and build confidence in their ability to think through problems and articulate their thinking. Likewise, asking for a variety of strategies for solving a problem helps students understand that risk-taking is desirable and lets them know that you take a genuine interest in their thinking. Encouraging students to ask each other questions about their strategies helps to create a classroom environment in which students learn to respect each other's thinking and feel safe sharing their own.

Class Building

At the beginning of the year in particular, it is important to help students develop a sense of identity and community as a class in order to support and develop a sense of cooperation. Students need many opportunities to learn about each other, to set norms for behavior, and to make decisions about their classroom. Activities such as developing a class name, logo, or handshake can lead to an "our classroom" feeling. This "class building" is an ongoing process; the spirit of community needs to be developed and supported throughout the year. Class-building activities are particularly important after a long vacation, after you have been absent for an extended period of time, after illness has kept many students home, or when you have an influx of new students. (Many ideas for class-building activities can be found in such resources as Graves's *A*

Part to Play, Moorman and Dishon's *Our Classroom*, Rhodes and McCabe's *The Nurturing Classroom*, and Gibbs and Allen's *Tribes*. See Additional Reading, p. 167.)

The physical setup of the room is also an important factor in creating an environment that supports cooperation. The arrangement should allow group members to have access to materials and to be able to communicate easily with each other. Sharing one desk or small table or sitting at two desks side-by-side are good arrangements for a pair; a small table or a cluster of desks work well for a group of four.

Forming Groups

You will need to make several decisions regarding group formation: the size of the groups, how to form them, and how long to keep them together. Most of the lessons in this volume are designed for pair work although there are several opportunities for students to work in groups of four as well. Working in pairs allows students to get to know each other, take turns, participate, and have time to share their thinking. Learning to cooperate is a developmental process and can be difficult for children, especially in the beginning of the year. They may, for example, have trouble sharing the work or listening to each other. Working in pairs provides an opportunity for students to learn and use these skills with just one other student.

The *Number Power* program suggests randomly grouping students in pairs that stay together for an entire unit. A major benefit of random assignment is that it gives several positive messages to students: there is no hidden agenda behind how you grouped them (such as choosing pairs based on student achievement); every student is considered a valuable group member; and everyone is expected to learn to work with everyone else. Random assignment also results in heterogeneous groupings, important for cooperative work, even though at times a pair may be homogenous in some way—for example, both partners may be girls. The following are several ways to randomly group students. (Other suggestions can be found in the Johnsons' *Circle of Learning*. See Additional Reading, p. 167.)

1. Have students find someone in the room with hands about the same size as theirs, or with eyes

of the same color, or someone who is wearing the same color.

2. Have students take a playing card or another object with a number on it and find someone else with the same number.

3. Have students take a card with an equation or short word problem on it and form a group with others who have an equation or word problem with the same solution. For example, one student who has the problem $10 + 15 =$ on his card might partner up with a student who has $20 + 5 =$ on her card.

4. Cut magazine pictures in half. Have each student pick a half and find the student with the other half.

Keeping pairs together for an entire unit provides an opportunity for students to develop and expand their interpersonal skills and their understanding of group interaction. Students learn to work through and learn from problems, and to build on successful methods of interaction. Working with the same partners over time also allows students to build on their mathematical discoveries and enhance their ability to explain their thinking and solutions to others.

Team Building

Each time new long-term pairs are formed, it is important to provide opportunities for students to get better acquainted, to develop a sense of identity as a team, and to begin to develop their working relationship. Each *Number Power* unit begins with a team-building activity that helps students label, discuss, and analyze behavior and that lays a foundation for their future pair or group work. Open-ended questions can draw students' attention to their interaction, to responsible behavior that helps their collaborative work, and to how they might solve problems that arise. Encourage students to talk about how they worked together and the problems they had; the cooperative skills they used; how they wish to treat each other; why it is important to be fair, caring, and responsible; and the ways they wish to work together the next time.

What Is My Role?

One of the main goals of cooperative group and pair work is encouraging children to do their own thinking and to take responsibility for their own learning. Your role is vital to the process of children becoming independent and interdependent learners. In addition to setting the environment for cooperation, this role includes planning and introducing the lesson, facilitating group work, helping students reflect, and helping them say good-bye. It also includes asking open-ended questions throughout the experience to individuals, pairs, groups, and the class to extend and help students verbalize their thinking.

Planning

Reading a *Number Power* unit (Overview and lessons) prior to implementation will help you make decisions about how to connect the lessons with students' previous mathematical experiences, and will alert you to the social values and group skills that might be emphasized throughout the unit. The group skills listed on the first page of each lesson are suggestions based on the type of student interaction that might occur in that lesson. (Listening skills, for example, might be the focus of a lesson in which students are explaining their thinking to others.) However, the developmental level of your students, their previous cooperative group experiences, and the level of cooperation they demonstrate may lead you to choose other skills as a focus. You might also wish to develop a theme for a unit, such as "communicating with others."

The following list of questions may help you as you plan. *Number Power* lessons incorporate suggestions for many of them.

- What are the important *mathematical concepts* of the lesson? How are they linked with previous work and long-term goals?
- What are some possible opportunities for supporting social, as well as mathematical, learning?
- Is the lesson *interesting, accessible,* and *challenging* for all students? What modifications are needed?
- What *room arrangement* will be best for the lesson?
- What *materials* will be needed for the lesson?

- How will time for *student discussion* and *work* be maximized?
- How will *interdependence* between partners be encouraged?
- How will the lesson provide opportunities for students to *make decisions* and *take responsibility* for their learning and behavior?
- What will you be looking for as you *observe* group work?
- What *open-ended questions* might extend students' thinking?
- How will *assessment* be linked with *instruction?*
- What are appropriate *extension activities* for pairs that finish early, or for the next day?

Introducing the Lesson

Many *Number Power* lessons begin with questions that ask students to reflect on previous lessons or experiences, or pose a problem for students to discuss. Such questions are often followed with discussion about an investigation or a problem that students will undertake and about group skills that might help them work effectively.

Discussing group skills at the beginning of the lesson provides students with models for positive interaction and with language to discuss their interaction. Vary the way these skills are discussed. You might choose, for example, to emphasize a skill such as sharing the work and then have students discuss what it means to share the work, how the work might be shared, how sharing the work might help their pair work, and how sharing the work relates to the values of being fair, caring, and responsible. You might ask pairs to discuss and choose skills that they think are important to the functioning of their pair, or ask students to discuss what they have learned about working together that will help them in this new lesson. At other times, students could role-play the activity and then with the class, discuss what they observed about the role-play and what cooperative skills they think might be particularly important to the work. For some lessons, you might decide not to discuss cooperative skills at all during the introduction. No matter how and when you choose to discuss the social emphases of the lesson and the group skills with students, it is important to remember that social understanding is constructed through many opportunities to work with others and reflect on their experience.

Facilitating Group Work

As students begin to work, observe each pair to be sure that students have understood the task and have no insurmountable problems. Then, focus on a few pairs, and observe each of them long enough to see what is really happening. This will provide you with information about students' ability to work together, their involvement in the activity, and their mathematical and social understanding. Such observation will also give you ideas for questions you might ask to help students define the problems they are investigating, solve interpersonal problems, take responsibility for their learning and behavior, and extend and informally assess their thinking.

If a pair is having difficulty, allow partners time to solve a problem themselves. If you decide to intervene, ask key questions to help them resolve the difficulty, rather than solving the problem for them or giving lengthy explanations. When you intervene to assess or extend thinking, try not to interrupt the flow of the pair work. Wait for a natural pause in the action. Ask open-ended questions that require progressively more thought or understanding.

Helping Students Reflect

Reflection on the mathematical and social aspects of pair work helps students develop their conceptual understanding, build on past learning experiences, and connect their experience to long-term learning goals. Asking open-ended questions before, during, and after pair work helps extend students' mathematical thinking and encourages them to consider such important issues as, "What does it mean to be responsible?" and "How did my behavior affect my partner?" *Number Power* lessons incorporate several methods to structure ongoing reflection, including pair discussion, writing, and whole-class discussions. Each *Number Power* unit ends with a transition lesson to provide students with an opportunity to reflect on their mathematical work and group interaction during the unit.

Helping Students Say Good-Bye

When it is time to disband pairs that have been working together for some time, it is important to provide opportunities for partners to express their feelings and to say good-bye. The transition lessons

at the end of each *Number Power* unit are designed
for this purpose. You may wish to use some other
parting activities, such as:

1. **Our Memories Bulletin Board.** Have partners
   draw favorite memories about their group work
   or about each other and then post them on a
   bulletin board labeled "Our Memories."

2. **Our Memory Books.** Have pairs make a book
   that includes work from their favorite investigations, comments from each partner about what
   they liked about the unit and working together,
   and a picture or drawing of the pair.

3. **Thank-You Letters.** Have partners draw thank-
   you pictures or write thank-you letters to each
   other expressing appreciation for something
   specific.

4. **Good-Bye Celebrations.** Have each pair plan a
   way to celebrate its work together.

(For ideas on parting or closing activities, see
Rhodes and McCabe's *The Nurturing Classroom*
and Gibbs and Allen's *Tribes*. See Additional
Reading, p. 167.)

Number Power Format

The *Number Power* program for Grade 2 consists of six units of seven to ten lessons each, designed to help students develop their understanding of the composition and decomposition of numbers, number meaning, place value concepts, and the relative magnitude of numbers. The units are also designed to help students better understand the meaning of operations and to develop reasonable strategies for carrying them out. The units are contained in two volumes with three units each; Volume 1: *Grouping, Place Value, and Informal Computation*; and Volume 2: *Informal Computation and Number Relationships*.

In Volume 1, Unit 1, students explore number patterns, counting by various groupings, and the meaning of numbers in data. In Volume 1, Unit 2, students build on their experiences in Unit 1 as they group and count by tens and hundreds, build place value understandings, and compute with multiples of ten and one hundred. In Volume 1, Unit 3, students continue to group and count while exploring the meaning of operations, particularly multiplication and division, and how they are related.

Volume 2, Unit 1 emphasizes building meaning about the number 100 and extending these understandings to numbers greater than 100. Students explore 100 as a quantity of objects, as a number that can be composed of and decomposed into other numbers, and as a benchmark for estimating and for exploring relative magnitude. In Volume 2, Unit 2, students practice mentally adding and subtracting with one- and two-digit numbers as they play cooperative partner games with dice, spinners, and various game boards. In Volume 2, Unit 3, students continue to develop addition and subtraction strategies as they solve problems, explain their own computation methods, and listen to the methods of others.

The *Number Power* program for Grade 2 is also designed to foster students' understanding of and commitment to the values of fairness, caring, and responsibility. The lessons in both volumes help students develop group skills, such as the ability to share the work and make decisions. Students are encouraged to take turns, explain their thinking clearly, and listen to each other. They reflect on ways to help each other, to give each other time to think, and to treat each other considerately. Throughout the units, students are encouraged to take responsibility for their learning and behavior and to reflect on how their behavior affects the work, others in the group, and themselves.

Unit Format

Each unit includes an Overview, a team-building lesson, conceptual lessons, and a transition lesson.

Overview

The Overview will acquaint you with the unit and offer suggestions for implementation. This section provides a synopsis of all the lessons, a discussion of the major mathematical concepts and social understandings that the lessons help students develop, and a list of all the materials you will need for the unit. The Overview also includes a discussion of informal assessment techniques you might use throughout the unit, ideas for ongoing activities, and a summary of the specific types of student writing opportunities in the unit.

Team-Building Lessons

Each unit begins with a team-building lesson. The focus of this lesson is to help partners become acquainted and to begin to develop a sense of identity as a pair. These lessons also provide opportunities for students to discuss and practice effective group skills. If you wish to engage students in additional team-building activities, consult *A Part to Play, Tribes, Our Classroom,* and *The Nurturing Classroom*, listed in Additional Reading, p. 167.

Conceptual Lessons

Subsequent lessons focus on developing and extending students' sense of number through a variety of cooperative problem-solving experiences. The lessons also provide opportunities for students to develop their abilities to work together effectively and to reflect on their mathematical and social experiences.

Transition Lessons

Each unit ends with a transition lesson that encourages students to reflect on their mathematical work throughout the unit and to make generalizations and connections. Transition lessons are also designed to encourage students to think about their interactions, their successes and problems, and the things they have learned that will help them when working together in the future.

In addition to this reflection, transition lessons allow students to express appreciation for each other and to celebrate their work together. After students have worked as a pair for a period of time, it may be difficult for them to face separation and move to a new group or partner. The transition lesson gives students a chance to make this break more easily by giving them time to acknowledge their attachment to one another and by providing ways to say good-bye.

Lesson Format

First Page

The first page provides you with the logistical information you need for the lesson.

Notice the lesson summary (A). Next to the summary you will often see an icon (B) which alerts you to the need for preparation prior to the lesson or to a lesson's special focus: team-building or transition.

The first page details the dual emphasis of the lesson. It lists the mathematical and social emphases (C and D), as well as the essential mathematical and social concepts of the lesson (E and F). (See "Planning," p. xiv, for a discussion about choosing group skills.)

On the first page you will also find a list of the materials specific to the lesson (G) and the suggested group size (H). *It is assumed that calculators and manipulative materials are available to students at all times for use at their discretion, and that the materials listed for students are available to groups or pairs in their work area at the start of the lesson, unless otherwise indicated in a unit or lesson.*

Interior Pages

Some lessons begin with a section titled Before the Lesson (I). This section suggests preliminary student activities or other preparations that you may need to undertake prior to the lesson.

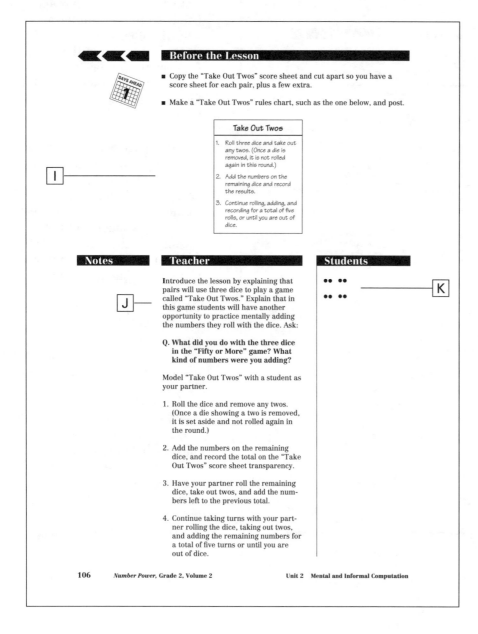

The lesson is divided into three columns. The center column (J) is the lesson plan itself and includes sample open-ended questions to probe and extend students' thinking.

The right column describes student work. It includes icons (K) that indicate how the students are grouped for each section of the lesson and descriptions of their cooperative work (L).

The left column provides notes and suggestions for you, as well as boxes that highlight important mathematical (M) and social (N) concepts as the focus of your open-ended questions in that part of the lesson. In some lessons this column also contains an assessment icon (O) accompanied by suggestions for informal assessment.

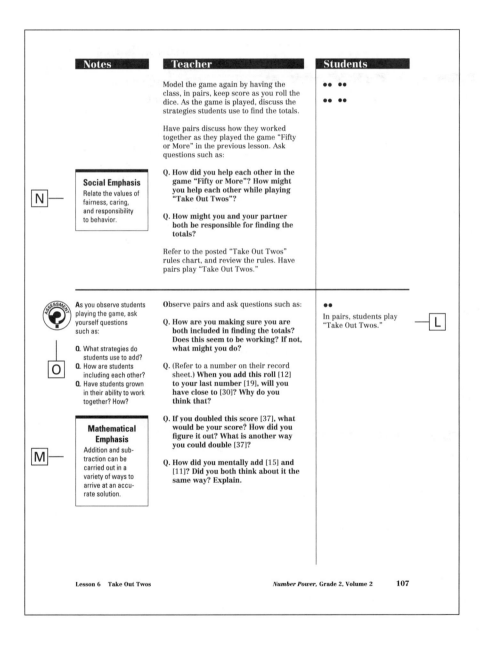

Notes

N—

Social Emphasis
Relate the values of fairness, caring, and responsibility to behavior.

O—

O. What strategies do students use to add?

O. How are students including each other?

O. Have students grown in their ability to work together? How?

M—

Mathematical Emphasis
Addition and subtraction can be carried out in a variety of ways to arrive at an accurate solution.

Teacher

Model the game again by having the class, in pairs, keep score as you roll the dice. As the game is played, discuss the strategies students use to find the totals.

Have pairs discuss how they worked together as they played the game "Fifty or More" in the previous lesson. Ask questions such as:

Q. How did you help each other in the game "Fifty or More"? How might you help each other while playing "Take Out Twos"?

Q. How might you and your partner both be responsible for finding the totals?

Refer to the posted "Take Out Twos" rules chart, and review the rules. Have pairs play "Take Out Twos."

Observe pairs and ask questions such as:

Q. How are you making sure you are both included in finding the totals? Does this seem to be working? If not, what might you do?

Q. (Refer to a number on their record sheet.) When you add this roll [12] to your last number [19], will you have close to [30]? Why do you think that?

Q. If you doubled this score [37], what would be your score? How did you figure it out? What is another way you could double [37]?

Q. How did you mentally add [15] and [11]? Did you both think about it the same way? Explain.

As you observe students playing the game, ask yourself questions such as:

Students

•• ••
•• ••

••
In pairs, students play "Take Out Twos." —L

Group Size Icons

Whole class icons

Teacher talks with the whole class, prior to grouping students, or after group work is complete.

Teacher talks with the whole class, already in groups of four.

Teacher talks with the whole class, already in pairs.

Student work icons

Students work in groups of four.

Students work in pairs.

Last Page— Extensions

Cooperative groups seldom finish their work at the same time. To help manage this and to further students' conceptual development, two additional types of activities are included at the end of each lesson.

The first, "For Pairs [or Groups] That Finish Early" (P), suggests activities for pairs to engage in as other pairs complete their lesson work. The second, "For the Next Day" (Q), further develops concepts or gives students more experience with the same concepts before moving on to the next lesson in the unit. Some of the activities foster students' social, as well as academic, learning.

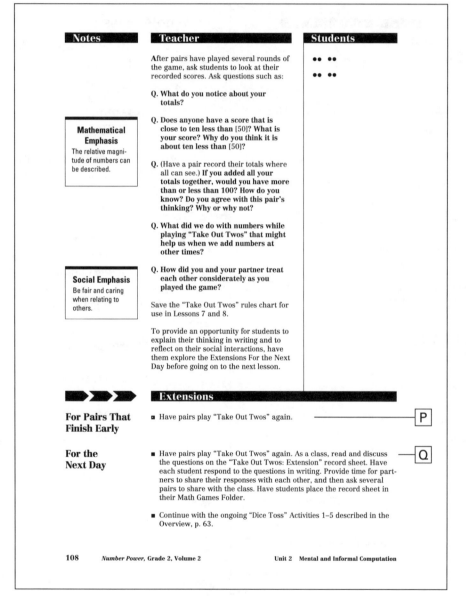

Notes	Teacher	Students
	After pairs have played several rounds of the game, ask students to look at their recorded scores. Ask questions such as:	•• •• •• ••
	Q. What do you notice about your totals?	
Mathematical Emphasis The relative magnitude of numbers can be described.	**Q.** Does anyone have a score that is close to ten less than [50]? What is your score? Why do you think it is about ten less than [50]?	
	Q. (Have a pair record their totals where all can see.) If you added all your totals together, would you have more than or less than 100? How do you know? Do you agree with this pair's thinking? Why or why not?	
	Q. What did we do with numbers while playing "Take Out Twos" that might help us when we add numbers at other times?	
Social Emphasis Be fair and caring when relating to others.	**Q.** How did you and your partner treat each other considerately as you played the game?	
	Save the "Take Out Twos" rules chart for use in Lessons 7 and 8.	
	To provide an opportunity for students to explain their thinking in writing and to reflect on their social interactions, have them explore the Extensions For the Next Day before going on to the next lesson.	

Extensions

For Pairs That Finish Early

▫ Have pairs play "Take Out Twos" again. ————— P

For the Next Day

■ Have pairs play "Take Out Twos" again. As a class, read and discuss the questions on the "Take Out Twos: Extension" record sheet. Have each student respond to the questions in writing. Provide time for partners to share their responses with each other, and then ask several pairs to share with the class. Have students place the record sheet in their Math Games Folder. ————— Q

■ Continue with the ongoing "Dice Toss" Activities 1–5 described in the Overview, p. 63.

Number Meaning and Relationships

Mathematical Development

This unit helps students understand the number 100 and extend this understanding to numbers greater than 100. Students explore 100 as a quantity of objects, compose and decompose 100 using other numbers, use 100 as a benchmark number to estimate, and explore questions about relative magnitude of numbers close to 100 or between 100 and 200. Students also begin to think about 25 and 50 as benchmark numbers and as numbers they can use to compose 100. They look for patterns in numbers 1 to 100 and see if these patterns extend into a larger numbers. They make estimates and mentally compute, taking many opportunities to verbalize and verify their strategies with each other.

Social Development

This unit provides opportunities for students to get to know each other and to begin to develop effective skills for working with others. Students are encouraged to listen to each other, take turns, and explain their thinking clearly. They find ways to help each other, reach agreement when they make joint decisions, and share the work in a fair way. They think about what it means to use materials in a responsible way. Students also have opportunities to analyze their behavior and interactions and reflect on how these affect others and their work. They discuss problems that occur and share ideas about effective ways to address these problems. Throughout the unit, students develop a "Working Together" chart.

Students are randomly assigned partners that work together throughout the unit. In Lesson 2, pairs interact with others pairs.

Mathematical Emphasis

Conceptually, experiences in this unit help students construct their understanding that

- Numbers can be composed and decomposed.

- Numbers can be used to describe quantities.

- The relative magnitude of numbers can be described.

- Making a reasonable estimate requires gathering and using information.

- Quantities of objects can be grouped and counted in a variety of ways.

- Addition and subtraction can be carried out in a variety of ways to arrive at an accurate solution.

- The same pattern can occur in a variety of settings.

Social Emphasis

Socially, experiences in this unit help students to

- Develop group skills.

- Take responsibility for learning and behavior.

- Analyze the effect of behavior on others and on the group work.

- Relate the values of fairness, caring, and responsibility to behavior.

- Analyze why it is important to be fair, caring, and responsible.

Lessons

This unit includes nine lessons and three ongoing activities: two charts (see "Working Together" chart and "Things We Know About 100" chart, p. 3) and a computation activity (see "Hundreds of Beans" activities, p. 3). The calendar icon indicates that some preparation is needed or that an experience is suggested for students prior to that lesson.

1. Hungry Ants!
(page 9)

Introductory team-building lesson in which pairs create and illustrate a new ending to the story, *One Hundred Hungry Ants*.

2. What About 100?
(page 15)

Exploration lesson in which pairs write statements about 100 and discuss their ideas with another pair.

3. Hundred Chart Exploration
(page 19)

Exploration lesson in which pairs locate numbers, identify patterns, and make other discoveries on the Hundred Chart.

4. One Hundred or More
(page 25)

Mental and informal computation lesson in which pairs mentally add with multiples of ten.

5. One Hundred Beans
(page 31)

Estimation and mental computation lesson in which pairs group and count beans using 50 and 100 as referents.

6. Four Steps to 100
(page 37)

Calculator lesson in which pairs find different ways to add four numbers to reach a total of 100.

7. Two-Hundred Chart Exploration
(page 43)

Exploration lesson in which pairs locate numbers, identify patterns, and make other discoveries on the Two-Hundred Chart.

8. Find Your Place
(page 49)

Relative magnitude lesson in which pairs compare numbers to referents such as 100, 125, 150, and 200.

9. Collections
(page 55)

Transition lesson in which pairs use collections brought from home to group, count, estimate, and mentally compute.

"Working Together" Chart

This ongoing activity provides opportunities for students to reflect on and record ways to work together with a partner and with the class. Before Lesson 1, make a chart entitled "Working Together." During Lessons 1, 2, 4, 6, and 9, students are encouraged to think about ways they worked well with a partner and contribute ideas to the chart. Although this chart is mentioned in only these lessons, add to it and discuss it whenever you feel it is appropriate. For example, you may want to begin a social studies lesson by referring to the chart and asking students to discuss ways to work together that will be important for that activity. Encourage students to suggest ideas for the chart at any time during the day.

"Things We Know About 100" Chart

In this ongoing activity, students contribute statements about the number 100 to a "Things We Know About 100" chart. The chart is introduced after Lesson 2 and revisited in Lessons 3, 5, and 9. This activity gives students opportunities to verbalize their understanding of the number 100, and provides a record of their learning. Students might make statements to show their understanding of number as quantity (for example, "I have 100 stickers in my collection"), of number composition (for example, "50 and 50 makes 100"), and of relative magnitude (for example, "99 is close to 100").

"Hundreds of Beans" Activities

Use these short, teacher-directed activities after Lesson 5 to help students count on to or count backward from 100, compute mentally using multiples of 100, and think about the relative magnitude of numbers. The activities use the bean bags (with 100 beans) that students will make at the end of Lesson 5.

■ Display one bean bag, and ask:

Q. Who remembers how many beans you put in each bag?

Place the bean bag and an additional small handful of beans on the overhead projector, and ask:

Q. How many beans are there on the overhead? How can we find out?

Point to the bag of 100 beans and count on from 100 in different ways to find the total. For example:

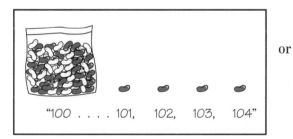
or
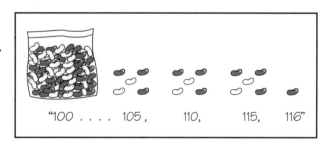

Repeat the activity several times using different counting on strategies and using more than one bag of 100 beans.

■ Display [two] bean bags, and ask:

Q. How many beans are there? How do you know?

Add [four] bean bags, and ask:

Q. How many beans are there now? How do you know?

■ Display [five] bean bags, and ask:

Q. If I take away [three] bean bags, how many beans are there? How do you know?

Continue adding and subtracting different numbers of bean bags and asking similar questions.

■ Display a bean bag, take some beans from the bag, and place the beans on the overhead projector. For example:

Ask:

Q. How many beans are left in the bag? How do you know?

Repeat the activity several times, removing a different number of beans each time.

Materials ▰▰▰▰▰▰▰▰▰▰▰▰▰▰▰▰▰▰▰▰▰▰▰▰▰▰▰▰▰▰

The materials needed for the unit are listed below. The first page of each lesson lists the materials specific to that lesson. Blackline masters for transparencies and group record sheets are included at the end of each lesson.

Throughout the unit, you will need an overhead projector and overhead pens, and students will need supplies such as counters, interlocking cubes, crayons, paper, and pencils. If possible, each pair should have a container with these supplies available to use at their discretion. In Lesson 6, students will need a calculator.

Teacher Materials
- Materials for forming pairs (Lesson 1)
- *One Hundred Hungry Ants* by Elinor J. Pinczes (Boston: Houghton Mifflin Co., 1993) (Lesson 1)
- 100 interlocking cubes (Lesson 1)
- Sheets of 12″ × 18″ drawing paper (Lesson 1)
- Chart paper (Lessons 1, 2, 4)
- Hundred Pocket Chart (Lessons 3, 7)
- 1–100 Pocket Chart cards (Lesson 3)
- Transparency of Hundred Chart (Lesson 3)
- Wooden cubes (Lesson 4)
- Adhesive dots (Lesson 4)
- Transparency of 1–120 Chart (Lesson 4)
- Transparent counters (Lessons 4, 7)
- Bowl of lima beans (Lesson 5)
- Sentence strip half (Lesson 5)
- Overhead calculator (Lesson 6)
- Blank transparency (Lesson 6)
- 101–200 Pocket Chart cards (Lesson 7)
- Transparency of Two-Hundred Chart (Lesson 7)
- Transparency of blank 10″ × 10″ grid (Lesson 7)
- 9″ × 12″ tagboard (Lesson 8)
- 5″ × 8″ index card (Lessons 8, 9)
- Resealable plastic bag for each student (Lesson 8)
- Adhesive labels (Lesson 8)
- "Family Letter" for each student (Lesson 8)
- 2 collection bags (Lesson 9)
- 12″ × 18″ construction paper (Lesson 9)

Student Materials
Each pair needs
- Hundred Chart (Lessons 3, 6, 7)
- Transparent counters (Lessons 3, 4, 7)
- 1–120 Chart (Lesson 4)
- Felt or construction paper mat (optional; Lesson 4)
- Paper bowl of lima beans (Lesson 5)
- 12″ × 18″ construction paper (optional; Lesson 5)
- Sentence strip halves (Lesson 5)
- Resealable plastic bag (Lesson 5)
- Calculator (Lesson 6)
- Two-Hundred Chart (Lessons 7, 8)
- 5″ × 8″ index card (Lessons 8, 9)

Each student needs
- 12″ × 18″ construction paper (Lesson 9)

Extension Materials
- Transparency of Two-Hundred Chart (Lesson 8)
- Transparency of blank 10″ × 10″ grid (Lesson 8)

Each pair needs
- Sentence strip halves (Lesson 5)
- Calculator (Lesson 6)
- Hundred Chart (Lesson 7)
- Two-Hundred Chart (Lessons 7, 8)
- 5″ × 8″ index card (Lesson 9)

Teaching Hints

- For Lesson 1, you will need the book *One Hundred Hungry Ants,* by Elinor J. Pinczes (Boston: Houghton Mifflin Company, 1993). If you do not have the book, see note on p. 11 for suggestions.

- In Lessons 3 and 7, it is suggested that you use a Hundred Pocket Chart. This type of pocket chart has one hundred clear plastic pockets that allow numeral cards to be visible when inserted. Numeral cards from 1–100 come with the chart, and 101–200 cards are available as a separate set. The pocket chart and numeral cards are available through catalogs and at teacher supply stores. If you do not have a Pocket Chart or numeral cards, you can use a blank 10 × 10 grid transparency (see Lesson 7) on the overhead projector instead.

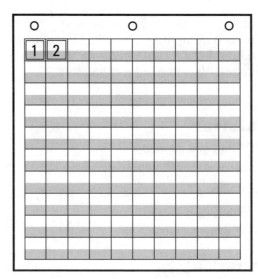

- Students use dice in Lesson 4. Provide time for students to explore rolling dice in a responsible manner before the lesson. To reduce the noise level, you might provide each pair with a felt mat or a piece of construction paper on which to roll the dice.

- Students use calculators in Lesson 6. If students' experience with calculators is limited, provide time for them to explore the calculator and discuss their discoveries before this lesson.

- Students are asked to bring in a collection of 80–120 objects for use in Lesson 9. Each collection should fit into the small resealable plastic bag they receive at the end of Lesson 8. For example, a collection might contain small rocks, bottle caps, or paper clips. You will need two collections of your own for demonstration purposes, plus several extra collection bags for students who are unable to bring a collection from home.

- In this unit, students are frequently asked to explain their thinking to their partners and to the class. Many lessons suggest that you ask follow-up questions to help students more fully explain or demonstrate their understanding. Recognize, however, that many students will have difficulty doing so, particularly at the beginning of the year. Provide many opportunities for students to talk about their thinking, to hear the thinking of others, and to use a variety of strategies to demonstrate their thinking, such as drawing pictures, showing their thinking using concrete objects, or verbalizing their solutions to a problem.

- Before each lesson, think about open-ended questions you might ask to extend and probe the thinking of your students. Decide which Extensions to have ready for pairs that finish early. After each lesson, review any Extensions students have not explored, and decide whether you want students to investigate these before going on to the next lesson.

Assessment Techniques

Before each lesson, select some of the suggested open-ended questions to ask your students to explore their mathematical and social understanding or develop questions of your own. Be ready to probe students' thinking during the lesson by asking follow-up questions that require them to explain further (for example, *How do you know? Say more about that. What do you mean by ___?*) Keep in mind that students' ability to clearly verbalize their thinking does not always match their conceptual understanding. Encourage students to communicate their thinking the best they can, perhaps helping them think about how they would explain their idea to a younger student, or encouraging them to use pictures, diagrams, or manipulatives. Remember that students' ability to verbalize their thinking improves with opportunities to practice over time.

Note that many lessons have an assessment section in the notes column with specific questions you can ask yourself as you observe your students. Whenever possible, record students' responses and compare them over time to assess growth in students' conceptual understanding. As you observe students throughout the unit, consider using the assessment questions below. Note change in students' conceptual understanding as well as their behavior; for example, *Does the student exhibit confidence in his or her own mathematical thinking? Is he or she able to persevere? Does the student give up easily, suggesting a belief that he or she lacks the ability to solve the problem? If so, does the student experience success and demonstrate more confidence as the unit progresses?*

Observe Individual Students Working

As you observe and listen to students, ask yourself questions such as:

> **Q. Can the student compose and decompose numbers in a variety of ways?**

Students who are developing good number sense can demonstrate flexibility in composing and decomposing numbers. For example, the number 100 can be composed in a great many ways: ten 10s, four 25s, two 50s, 98 + 2, 45 + 15 + 30 + 30, etc. In this unit, activities such as "One Hundred Beans" and "Four Steps to 100" reinforce students' ability to think about addends that make 100, or smaller numbers that 100 can be decomposed into.

> **Q. Is the student able to recognize and describe patterns in the numbers 1 to 100? Can the student recognize these same patterns in larger numbers?**

Students find many patterns in numbers from 1 to 100, particularly when presented with these numbers in the form of a Hundred Chart. They may notice patterns such as counting by tens from a given number as they move vertically down a column, or all the ones digits in a column being the same number. Over time, students should begin to generalize some of their observations, leading to understandings about the number system as a whole. In this unit, students have opportunities to explore the connections between the numbers 1–100 and larger numbers as they study and compare the Hundred and Two-Hundred Charts to each other.

Reflect on Your Role as Teacher

As you reflect on your role in each lesson, consider the following questions:

> **Q. Did I ask open-ended questions and allow enough wait time for students? Did I provide opportunities for students to discuss their thinking with each other before sharing with the class? How? How did I encourage students to contribute to the class discussion? Did I listen to their responses and probe their thinking when it seemed appropriate? How?**

Q. Did I allow time for students to reason through and explain their own strategies, or did I inadvertently impose my thinking? Did I ask open-ended questions? Did I encourage a variety of responses? How did I handle the unexpected?

Q. What understandings have students developed through these experiences? What additional experiences would enhance students' understanding?

Student Writing

Throughout the unit, students are asked to verbalize their thinking and, at times, to record their thinking in writing. Students write a new ending to a number story in Lesson 1. In Lesson 2, students write statements about 100.

Hungry Ants!

Students get to know each other as they use numbers to create a new ending to the story *One Hundred Hungry Ants*. This lesson may take more than one class period.

Team Builder Emphasis

In this lesson, students

- Get to know their partner.
- Begin to develop an effective working relationship.
- Think about ways to show 100.

Students add to their understanding that

- Numbers can be used to describe quantities.
- Numbers can be composed and decomposed.

Social Emphasis

In this lesson, students

- Make decisions.
- Listen to others.
- Reach agreement.

Students continue to

- Develop group skills.
- Analyze why it is important to be fair, caring, and responsible.

Group Size: 2

Teacher Materials

- Materials for forming pairs (see Before the Lesson)
- *One Hundred Hungry Ants,* by Elinor J. Pinczes
- 100 interlocking cubes (see Before the Lesson)
- Sheets of 12″ × 18″ drawing paper (see Before the Lesson)
- Sample accordion book (see Before the Lesson)
- "Working Together" chart (see Before the Lesson)

Student Materials

Each pair needs

- Crayons or markers

Extension Materials

Each pair needs

- Paper and a pencil

■ Decide how you will form pairs to work together during the unit (see Forming Groups, p. xiii, for random-grouping suggestions). Prepare any materials needed.

■ Cut sheets of 12″ × 18″ drawing paper in half lengthwise to create 6″ × 18″ sheets. You will need one 6″ × 18″ sheet for a sample accordion book, one for use in the lesson, and one for each pair.

■ Use one 6″ × 18″ sheet to make an accordion book to use for demonstration purposes. Fold it in fourths, and write and illustrate a new ending for *One Hundred Hungry Ants*. Include numbers in your new ending. One example of a new ending might be:

| One little ant turned and said, "What do I smell?" | 99 ants turned and sniffed. "Another picnic! Down the way!" | "Off we go! Marching in 10 rows!" | 100 hungry ants ate until they were full! A hey and a hi dee ho! |

■ Put together ten rods of ten interlocking cubes each.

■ Title a sheet of chart paper "Working Together" and post.

Notes	Teacher	Students
Be sure partners know each other's names.	**R**andomly assign pairs. Explain that pairs will work together for several weeks as they help each other explore the number 100 and numbers greater than 100. Ask:	•• •• •• ••

Q. Why do you think 100 might be an important number to get to know?

Q. Does 100 seem like a big number or a small number? Why do you think so?

If you do not have the book *One Hundred Hungry Ants*, consider telling the story to your class to set a context for this lesson. In this story, 100 ants march off to a nearby picnic. Because marching in single file seems too slow, they try marching in two rows of 50, four rows of 25, and eventually ten rows of 10. By the time they finish organizing themselves, they have missed the picnic! In this lesson students will have an opportunity to write a different ending for the ants.

Mathematical Emphasis

Numbers can be composed and decomposed.

Show the book *One Hundred Hungry Ants* by Elinor J. Pinczes and explain that in this story, some ants go on a picnic. Ask partners to tell each other about a time they have been on a picnic, or what they would bring on a picnic if they were planning one.

Read aloud *One Hundred Hungry Ants*. First in pairs, then as a class, discuss:

Q. How were numbers used in the story? Explain.

Use the interlocking cubes to demonstrate the ants marching in two rows of 50. Ask questions such as:

Q. If the ants marched in four rows, would there by more or fewer ants in each row? How do you know?

Q. What is another way the ants marched in rows in the story? Could they have marched in rows in any other way?

Q. If the story continued, what might happen next? Explain. What is another way to change the ending?

Q. How might you use numbers in a new ending for the story?

Show the sample accordion book to the class and read aloud your new ending. Point out the use of numbers in your ending. Explain that pairs will work together to make an accordion book like your sample book, writing and illustrating a new ending to the story that uses numbers to tell what happened to the hundred hungry ants.

Notes	Teacher	Students

Social Emphasis
Analyze why it is important to be fair, caring, and responsible.

Discuss how partners might work together by asking questions such as:

•• ••

•• ••

Q. **How might you make decisions about the new ending to the story? Why is it important to make decisions together?**

Q. **Why is it important to listen to each other's ideas?**

Q. **How can you each take responsibility for the work?**

Distribute a sheet of 6″ × 18″ drawing paper to each pair, and ask them to fold the paper in fourths. Have pairs make an accordion book and then create and illustrate a new ending.

As you observe students, ask yourself questions such as:

Q. How are students making decisions about the ending? Does that seem to be working for them?

Q. How are students incorporating numbers in their new ending?

Observe pairs and ask questions such as:

Q. **How are you making decisions about your new ending? How is that working for you?**

Q. **How do you know your partner is listening to you?**

Q. **How are you using numbers in your new ending?**

••

In pairs, students make an accordion book and then create and illustrate a new ending to the story that uses numbers to tell what happens to the 100 hungry ants.

Students may use numbers in a variety of ways to tell what happens to the 100 ants. For example:

■ 75 ants find one picnic and 25 ants find another.
■ The ants march home in 25 rows of 4.

Have several pairs read their new ending to the class. Ask:

Q. **Does anyone have a question about this pair's ending?**

Q. **How did this pair use numbers in their ending?**

•• ••

•• ••

Social Emphasis
Develop group skills.

Refer to the "Working Together" chart. Explain that during the next several weeks, pairs will think about what helps them work together. Ask students to think about how they worked with their partner and what helped them work well together. As students offer suggestions, list the ideas on the chart. Ask questions such as:

Q. **One suggestion on our list is** [make decisions in a fair way]. **Who would like to tell us how you** [made decisions fairly] **today?**

Q. **Another idea is** [take turns]. **When did you** [take turns] **with your partner today? How did that help you?**

You may wish to display the accordion books on a bulletin board, or place them in a class library or math center.

Save the "Working Together" chart for use in the upcoming lessons in the unit.

Extensions

For Pairs That Finish Early

■ Have pairs solve this problem and explain their thinking in writing:

   How many ways could our class of [32] **students march in rows to a picnic?**

For the Next Day

■ Continue with the next lesson, "What About 100?"

What About 100?

Pairs brainstorm and write statements about the quantity 100 and discuss their ideas with another pair. The groups of four each choose two statements to contribute to a "Things We Know About 100" chart.

Mathematical Emphasis

In this lesson, students

- Describe the quantity 100 in a variety of ways.

Students add to their understanding that

- Numbers can be used to describe quantities.
- Numbers can be composed and decomposed.

Social Emphasis

In this lesson, students

- Make decisions.
- Listen to others.
- Reach agreement.
- Share the work.

Students continue to

- Develop group skills.
- Relate the values of fairness, caring, and responsibility to behavior.

Group Size: 2, then 4

Teacher Materials

- Chart paper
- "Working Together" chart (from Lesson 1)

Student Materials

Each pair needs

- Paper and a pencil

Extension Materials

Each pair needs

- Paper and a pencil

Notes	Teacher	Students

Students

•• ••

•• ••

Title a sheet of chart paper "Things We Know About 100," and post. Explain that in this lesson students will continue to explore and get to know the number 100. Ask:

Q. What do we already know about 100?

For example, students might say:

- "99 is close to 100."
- "50 and 50 makes 100."
- "100 pennies make $1.00."
- "My great-grandma is going to be 100 years old."

First in pairs, then as a class, have students brainstorm and share several ideas. Record students' ideas on the chart. Explain that pairs will work together to discuss other things they know about 100 and to record their ideas on a sheet of paper.

Refer to the "Working Together" chart and review the listed ideas. Ask questions such as:

Q. What ideas on the chart might help you and your partner work together in a fair way?

Social Emphasis
Relate the values of fairness, caring, and responsibility to behavior.

Q. What are some ways you can make decisions together about the statements to be recorded? Are these fair ways to make decisions? Why?

Ask pairs to first brainstorm and list several statements about the number 100.

At this point, you might want to take some notes of your observations and students' statements as these can serve as a preassessment of students' knowledge of 100 prior to experiencing the unit.

Observe pairs working and ask questions such as:

Q. Tell me about this statement.

Q. Why is it important to listen to your partner?

Q. How are you sharing the work?

Q. How are you deciding who will record each statement? Does this seem like a fair way?

••

In pairs, students brainstorm and list several statements about the number 100.

Notes	Teacher	Students

Explain that pairs will share their statements with another pair. Then, in groups of four, students will agree on the accuracy of each statement, revise statements if necessary, and agree on two statements to share with the class. Have each pair join another pair to make a group of four. Before groups begin to work, discuss questions such as:

Social Emphasis
Develop group skills.

Q. **What do you know about working with a partner that will help you work as a group of four?**

Q. **How can you be sure you include everyone?**

Observe students and ask questions such as:

Q. **What do you notice about your statements? How are they alike? How are they different?**

Q. (Point to a statement.) **How do you know that this statement is true? How do you know that everyone agrees?**

Q. **How are you and your partner showing the other pair in your group that you are listening to their statements?**

Q. **How are you agreeing on the statements to share with the class? How does that seem to be working?**

In groups, students

1. Share their statements about 100 with each other.

2. Agree on the acuracy of each statement, revise if necessary, and agree on two of the statements to report to the class.

Mathematical Emphasis
Numbers can be used to describe quantities.

Have groups report their statements about 100 to the class. As groups report, record the statements on the "Things We Know About 100" chart. Ask questions such as:

Q. (Refer to a group's statement.) **Do you agree with this group that** [all the hands and feet in our classroom equal 100]? **Why or why not?**

Q. **What questions do you have for this group?**

Notes	Teacher	Students

Teacher

Q. Did any other group have a similar statement? Explain.

Students

:: ::
:: ::

Help students reflect on the lesson by asking questions such as:

Q. How is working in a group of four different from working as a pair? What did you like about working together in a group of four? What was hard about working in a group of four?

Q. How did you come to agreement about the statements you reported to the class? What did you like about how you reached agreement? What might you do differently the next time?

Q. What ideas could we add to the "Working Together" chart?

If appropriate, share some of your observations of the positive interactions and problems you noted as students worked. Have students suggest ways the problems might be handled the next time they work together.

Save the "Things We Know About 100" chart and the "Working Together" chart for use in future lessons in this unit.

Extensions

For Groups That Finish Early

- Have groups brainstorm and write sentences about where they might find about 100 of something. For example, students might write, "There are about 100 students in three second grade classes," or "There might be about 100 pencils in the classroom." Have groups share their statements with the class.

For the Next Day

- If groups have not done the Extension For Groups That Finish Early, have them do so.

- Continue with the next lesson, "Hundred Chart Exploration."

Hundred Chart Exploration

Pairs use the Hundred Chart to locate numbers, look for patterns, and make observations. They then share their findings with the class.

Mathematical Emphasis

In this lesson, students

- Explore the Hundred Chart.
- Informally add and subtract.
- Identify patterns.

Students add to their understanding that

- Numbers can be composed and decomposed.
- The relative magnitude of numbers can be described.

Social Emphasis

In this lesson, students

- Explain their thinking.
- Listen to others.
- Share the work.

Students continue to

- Develop group skills.
- Analyze the effect of behavior on others and on the group work.

Group Size: 2

Teacher Materials

- Hundred Pocket Chart (see Overview, p. 6)
- 1–100 Pocket Chart cards
- Transparency of Hundred Chart
- "Things We Know About 100" chart (from Lesson 2)

Student Materials

Each pair needs

- Hundred Chart
- Transparent counter
- Paper and pencil

Review the previous lesson by asking:

Q. What are some things you found out about the number 100 when we made and shared our statements?

Hang the empty Hundred Pocket Chart. As students identify the numbers, have them place the cards into the pocket chart.

Explain that students will continue to think about 100 and numbers up to 100, and also look for patterns in numbers up to 100. Refer to the empty Hundred Pocket Chart. First in pairs, then as a class, discuss questions such as:

Q. (Point to the empty space in the upper left hand corner of the chart.) **If the numbers on this chart start with one** (put the "1" card into that space), **what number would be in this space** (point to the empty space to the right of 1)? **How do you know?**

Q. (Point to the empty space for 10.) **What number would be in this space? How do you know?** (Point to the empty space for 20.) **What number would be in this space? How did you decide?**

Q. (Point to the empty space in the lower right hand corner of the chart.) **What number would be in this space? How do you know?**

Q. **Where would 50 be on this chart? Explain.**

Put the number 5 in the appropriate space, and point to the empty space for 15. Ask:

Q. **What number would go here? What do you add to 5 to get 15? Explain. Where would 25 be located on this chart? How do you know?**

Q. **We are starting to fill in a Hundred Chart. Why do you think it is called a Hundred Chart?**

Distribute a copy of the Hundred Chart to each pair. Explain that pairs will explore the Hundred Chart, looking for patterns and other interesting observations they would like to share with the class.

| **Notes** | **Teacher** | **Students** |

As you observe students, ask yourself questions such as:

Q. Are students noticing patterns on the chart? What patterns do they see?

Q. How are students verbalizing their discoveries?

Q. What evidence do you see of students working well together?

Observe pairs working and ask questions such as:

Q. What are you noticing about the Hundred Chart? What would you like to report later to the class?

Q. How do you know your partner is listening to you? Why is that important?

•●

In pairs, students explore the Hundred Chart and get ready to report patterns they noticed and other interesting observations.

Show the Hundred Chart transparency on the overhead projector. Ask several pairs to share their discoveries about the chart. As pairs report, have them use the Hundred Chart transparency to demonstrate their thinking. Ask questions such as:

Q. Did anything surprise you? Explain.

Q. What patterns did you discover?

After several pairs have shared, provide each pair with a transparent counter. Ask pairs to look at their Hundred Chart and follow your directions:

Q. Place your counter on the number 16. How did you find 16?

Q. Place your counter on a number close to 50. Where did you place your counter? Why do you think [46] is close to 50?

Q. Place your counter on the number that is 10 more than [23]. What number did you cover with your counter? Explain. What number is 20 more than [23]? How do you know?

Q. Place your counter on the number that is 10 less than [84]. What number did you cover with your counter? Explain.

Q. What else might we add to our "Things We Know About 100" chart?

•● •●
•● •●

Mathematical Emphasis

The relative magnitude of numbers can be described.

Notes	**Teacher**	**Students**

Teacher

Add students' suggestions to the "Things We Know About 100" chart.

Help students reflect on their work together by asking questions such as:

Q. **Think about how the class worked together today. What went well? What caused problems? What might we do differently next time?**

Q. **Think about how you and your partner worked together today. What went well? How did that help you?**

Save the "Things We Know About 100" chart for use in future lessons in the unit.

Notes

Social Emphasis
Analyze the effect of behavior on others and on the group work.

Students

•• ••

•• ••

For the Next Day

Extensions

■ Continue with the next lesson, "One Hundred or More."

Hundred Chart

1	2	3	4	5	6	7	8	9	10
11	12	13	14	15	16	17	18	19	20
21	22	23	24	25	26	27	28	29	30
31	32	33	34	35	36	37	38	39	40
41	42	43	44	45	46	47	48	49	50
51	52	53	54	55	56	57	58	59	60
61	62	63	64	65	66	67	68	69	70
71	72	73	74	75	76	77	78	79	80
81	82	83	84	85	86	87	88	89	90
91	92	93	94	95	96	97	98	99	100

One Hundred or More

Pairs mentally add numbers to 100 or more as they play a game in which they use a die marked 1, 2, 5, 10, 10, and 20.

DAYS AHEAD
1

Mathematical Emphasis

In this lesson, students

- Mentally add with multiples of ten.
- Subtract to find the difference between two numbers.

Students add to their understanding that

- Numbers can be composed and decomposed.
- Addition and subtraction can be carried out in a variety of ways to arrive at an accurate solution.
- The relative magnitude of numbers can be described.

Social Emphasis

In this lesson, students

- Share the work.
- Take turns.
- Use materials responsibly.
- Reach agreement.

Students continue to

- Develop group skills.
- Analyze why it is important to be fair, caring, and responsible.
- Analyze the effect of behavior on others and on the group work.

Group Size: 2

Teacher Materials

- Die made with wooden cube and adhesive dots (see Before the Lesson)
- "One Hundred or More" rules chart (see Before the Lesson)
- Transparency of 1–120 Chart
- Transparent counter
- "Working Together" chart (from Lesson 1)

Student Materials

Each pair needs

- 1–120 Chart
- Die and mat (see Before the Lesson)
- Transparent counter
- Paper and a pencil

Extension Materials

Each pair needs

- "One Hundred or More" game materials

■ Make a die for each pair with the following numbers on the faces: 1, 2, 5, 10, 10, 20. To make the dice, write the numbers on adhesive dots and place the dots on the cubes.

■ Make a "One Hundred or More" rules chart, such as the one below, and post.

One Hundred or More

1. Partner 1—Roll the die and place a marker on the number rolled.

2. Partner 2—Roll the die, add the number to the first number rolled, and move the marker to the total.

3. Take turns rolling the die, adding the number rolled to the total, and moving the marker until 100 or more is reached.

4. Record the final score.

■ If students have not had much experience using a die, have them explore how to roll a die in a quiet and responsible manner. In order to diminish the noise of rolling dice, you may want to provide a felt mat or a piece of construction paper for each pair.

Notes

Teacher

Introduce the lesson by asking pairs to discuss what they discovered about the Hundred Chart in the previous lesson. Ask questions such as:

Q. What did you discover about the numbers on the Hundred Chart?

Q. Some students use the Hundred Chart as a tool to help them in math. How could you use the Hundred Chart?

Show the 1–120 Chart transparency on the overhead projector. First in pairs, then as a class, discuss questions such as:

Q. What do you notice about this chart?

Q. How is the 1–120 Chart like the Hundred Chart? How is it different?

Students

•• ••

•• ••

Q. **What number is 10 more than the number [33]? If you have a counter on [33], is there a way to add 10 without counting by ones? Explain.**

Q. **What is a number that is 10 less than [87]? How do you know? [20] more? Explain.**

Explain that pairs will continue to explore the numbers on the 1–120 Chart by using a special die to play a game called "One Hundred or More." Show a sample die, and explain that this die has 1, 2, 5, 10, 10, and 20 on its faces.

Explain that the object of the game is to roll the die, add the numbers rolled, and move a counter on the 1–120 Chart until 100 or more is reached. Model the game with a student as your partner:

1. Roll the die. Read aloud the number rolled and place the transparent counter on the number rolled.

2. Have your partner roll the die, read aloud the number, and together add the number to the number rolled previously. Agree on the sum and move the counter to the sum.

3. Continue to take turns with your partner rolling, adding, agreeing, and moving the counter until 100 or more is reached.

4. Record your ending score on a sheet of paper.

Have pairs play the game once as you roll the die for the class. When 100 or more is reached, ask pairs to record their total on a sheet of paper.

First in pairs, then as a class, have students discuss questions such as:

Q. **What is helping you and your partner work together well?**

Q. **How are you using the materials in a responsible way? Why is that important?**

As you and your partner add the roll of the die to the previous total and move the counter, verbalize how to use your knowledge of the Hundred Chart to move the counter. For example, if the counter is on 33 and the roll is 10, the counter could be moved down one space to 43 instead of starting on 33 and counting to 43 by ones.

Social Emphasis
Analyze why it is important to be fair, caring, and responsible.

Notes	Teacher	Students
	Q. (Refer to the "Working Together" chart.) **Is there an idea on the "Working Together" chart that might help you and your partner play this game?** Refer pairs to the posted "One Hundred or More" rules chart and have pairs play the game several times.	•• •• •• ••

(ASSESSMENT) As you observe students, as yourself questions such as:

Q. Are students using their knowledge of the Hundred Chart to move the counter? Are they counting by tens or ones?

Q. How are students working together? Are they sharing the work and the materials? How?

Observe pairs and ask questions such as:

Q. Your counter is on [64]. Where will you move the counter if you roll 10? How do you know? If you roll 20? Explain.

Q. Your counter is on [82]. How many points do you need to reach 100? How do you know?

Q. How are you sharing the work? Is that fair? Why?

Q. How are you agreeing on where to move your counter?

••

In pairs, students play "One Hundred or More."

After pairs have played the game several times, ask questions such as:

Q. What do you notice about your scores?

Q. What is your highest score? Lowest? What is the difference between your highest and lowest score?

Q. Look at your highest score. What would the score be if you had 10 more? How do you know? 10 less? Explain.

•• ••

•• ••

Mathematical Emphasis

The relative magnitude of numbers can be described.

Notes	**Teacher**	**Students**

Help partners reflect on how they played the game together by asking questions such as:

•• ••

•• ••

Q. **What did you like about how you worked together? Why?**

Q. **What problems did you have? How did that affect your work together? How did the problems make you feel?**

Q. **Did you and your partner use any of the ideas on the "Working Together" chart? Which ones? How did that help?**

Extensions

For Pairs That Finish Early

■ Have pairs play "One Hundred or More" again.

For the Next Day

■ Continue with the next lesson, "One Hundred Beans."

1–120 Chart

1	2	3	4	5	6	7	8	9	10
11	12	13	14	15	16	17	18	19	20
21	22	23	24	25	26	27	28	29	30
31	32	33	34	35	36	37	38	39	40
41	42	43	44	45	46	47	48	49	50
51	52	53	54	55	56	57	58	59	60
61	62	63	64	65	66	67	68	69	70
71	72	73	74	75	76	77	78	79	80
81	82	83	84	85	86	87	88	89	90
91	92	93	94	95	96	97	98	99	100
101	102	103	104	105	106	107	108	109	110
111	112	113	114	115	116	117	118	119	120

One Hundred Beans

Pairs group, count, record, and add the number of beans in each of four handfuls using 50 and 100 as referents.

DAYS AHEAD
1

Mathematical Emphasis

In this lesson, students

- Group and count objects by tens.
- Use 50 and 100 as referents.
- Informally add and subtract.

Students add to their understanding that

- Making a reasonable estimate requires gathering and using information.
- Numbers can be composed and decomposed.
- Numbers can be used to describe quantities.
- Quantities of objects can be grouped and counted in a variety of ways.

Social Emphasis

In this lesson, students

- Use materials responsibly.
- Share the work.
- Listen to others.
- Explain their thinking.

Students continue to

- Develop group skills.
- Relate the values of fairness, caring, and responsibility to behavior.

Group Size: 2

Teacher Materials

- Paper bowl of lima beans (see Before the Lesson)
- Sentence strip half (see Before the Lesson)
- "Things We Know About 100" chart (from Lesson 2)

Student Materials

Each pair needs

- Paper bowl of lima beans (see Before the Lesson)
- 12" x 18" sheet of construction paper (optional; see Before the Lesson)
- Sentence strip halves (see Before the Lesson)
- Resealable plastic bag

Extension Materials

Each pair needs

- Their paper bowl of lima beans
- Sentence strip halves

We have 23 beans in our first handful.

If my handful has about the same number, we will have about 50 beans. That's half of 100!

Number Power, Grade 2, Volume 2

■ You will need one paper bowl of approximately 130 lima beans for yourself and one for each pair.

■ Cut the sentence strips in half. You will need one half for yourself, two halves for each pair, and extra halves for Extensions (see Extensions For Pairs That Finish Early). Fold each half-strip into fourths, as shown:

■ You might want to provide a sheet of 12" x 18" construction paper for each pair to use as a workmat on which to organize their beans.

Notes	**Teacher**	**Students**
	Introduce the lesson by showing your paper bowl of lima beans. Take a small handful of beans and place them on the overhead projector. Ask:	●● ●● ●● ●●

Teacher

Introduce the lesson by showing your paper bowl of lima beans. Take a small handful of beans and place them on the overhead projector. Ask:

Q. Do you think there are more than or fewer than 25 beans in my handful? Explain.

Group and count the beans by tens. Ask:

Q. How many beans were in my handful? How many more handfuls might I need if I want 50 beans? How do you know? 100 beans?

Explain that pairs will take four handfuls of beans from their own bowl and try to get as close as possible to a total of 100 beans. Model the activity with a student as your partner:

1. Take a handful of beans from the bowl, group and count them by tens, and record the total in the first section of the sentence strip. Have your partner do the same, recording his or her handful in the next section of the strip. For example:

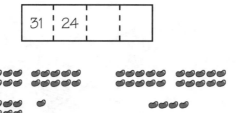

Ask:

Q. So far do we have more than or fewer than 50 beans? How do you know? How many [more/fewer] **than 50 beans do we have?**

Put any single beans that you and your partner may have together. For example:

2. With your partner, decide if you will need more or fewer than 50 additional beans to have 100, and discuss what size handfuls each of you should take next.

Keep the beans from the first two handfuls nearby while taking the second set of handfuls.

3. Take another handful from the bowl, group and count the beans by tens, and record the number in the third section of the strip. Have your partner do the same, recording his or her handful in the last section of the strip. For example:

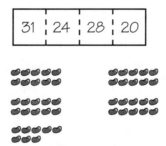

Ask:

Mathematical Emphasis

Making a reasonable estimate requires gathering and using information.

Q. Do you think we have more than or fewer than 100 beans altogether? Why?

4. Group all four handfuls together, count the beans, and record the total on the back of the strip. For example:

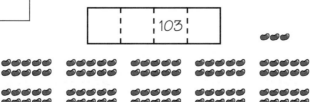

Notes	**Teacher**	**Students**

<table>
<tr>
<td></td>
<td>Ask:</td>
<td>•• ••
•• ••</td>
</tr>
</table>

Notes:

You may want to model the activity more than once.

Students might say:

- It could be a problem if one partner always takes a big handful, because to get close to 100 the other partner might always have to take a small handful.
- It could be a problem if partners don't listen to each other and agree on the size of their second handfuls before taking them.

Teacher:

Ask:

Q. **If we want to get closer to 100, what might we do differently next time?**

As a class, discuss questions such as:

Q. **What problems might pairs have doing this activity? If you have a problem, what could you do to solve it so no one's feelings get hurt or so the problem doesn't interfere with your work?**

Review the steps of the activity, and remind pairs that the goal is to try to get as close as possible to 100 beans by taking four handfuls. Ask pairs to do the activity twice.

Notes:

As you observe pairs, ask yourself questions such as:

Q. When students are combining the handfuls, are they counting by ones or tens?

Q. When students are deciding whether they need more or fewer than 50 additional beans to make 100, are they taking into account whether they have more or fewer than 50 beans already?

Q. How are students working together? Have they shown improvement in their ability to interact effectively? How?

Teacher:

Observe pairs and ask questions such as:

Q. (Point to the first two numbers on a sentence strip.) **About how many beans do you have? How do you know? About how many more beans do you need to have 100? Explain.**

Q. **What do you think would happen if your first handfuls are very big or very small?**

Q. (After a pair has done the activity once.) **What do you want to do [the same/differently] next time to get closer to 100? Why?**

Q. **What would you say about how you are working together? How does that make you feel? How is it affecting your work?**

Students:

••   In pairs, students

1. Each take a handful of beans, group and count them by tens, and record the total on a sentence strip.

2. Decide if they will need more or fewer than 50 additional beans to make 100.

3. Each take another handful of beans and repeat the activity.

4. Group all four handfuls together, and find and record the total on the back of the sentence strip.

5. Repeat the activity.

A cooperative structure such as "Think, Pair, Share" (see p. xii) can provide opportunities for all students to reflect on a problem before discussing their thinking.

Social Emphasis

Relate the values of fairness, caring, and responsibility to behavior.

Ask pairs to look at their recorded numbers. Ask questions such as:

Q. Did anyone get close to 100 beans? What was your total? How close did you get to 100 beans?

Q. What was your [lower/lowest] total? About how many more beans would you need to have 100? How do you know?

Q. Did any pair get exactly 100 beans? How many did you have in each of your handfuls? Did any other pair get exactly 100 beans?

Q. What might we add to the "Things We Know About 100" chart?

Add students' suggestions to the "Things We Know About 100" chart. Help students reflect on their work together by asking questions such as:

Q. How is working with a partner different from working alone? When you work alone, what things do you have to think about or do to be responsible? When you work with a partner, what things do you need to think about or do to be responsible or fair?

Have pairs fill a resealable plastic bag with 100 lima beans from this activity. Collect the bags for use in Extensions For the Next Day. Collect the sentence strips for use in Lesson 6. Save the "Things We Know About 100" chart for use in Lesson 9.

•• ••

•• ••

Extensions

For Pairs That Finish Early

■ Have pairs repeat the activity using another sentence strip.

For the Next Day

■ Begin the ongoing "Hundreds of Beans" activities described in the Overview, p. 3.

Four Steps to 100

Students find different ways to add four numbers to reach a total of 100 by playing a calculator game.

DAYS AHEAD
2

Mathematical Emphasis

In this lesson, students

- Estimate and use a calculator to compute informally.

Students add to their understanding that

- Numbers can be composed and decomposed.
- Making a reasonable estimate requires gathering and using information.

Social Emphasis

In this lesson, students

- Make decisions.
- Explain their thinking.
- Share the work.
- Use materials responsibly.

Students continue to

- Develop group skills.
- Take responsibility for learning and behavior.

Group Size: 2

Teacher Materials

- Sentence strip halves with recorded numbers (from Lesson 5)
- Overhead calculator
- Blank transparency and a marker
- "Working Together" chart (from Lesson 1)

Student Materials

Each pair needs

- Calculator
- Paper and a pencil
- Access to Hundred Chart (from Lesson 3)

Extension Materials

Each pair needs

- Calculator
- Paper and a pencil

■ If students' prior experience with the calculator is limited, provide time before this lesson for them to individually explore the calculator and to discuss what they discover.

Notes	**Teacher**	**Students**

Teacher

Introduce the lesson by reviewing the "One Hundred Beans" activity from Lesson 5. Hold up a sentence strip from that lesson with only two numbers showing. For example:

First in pairs, then as a class, have students discuss questions such as:

Q. Did this pair have more than or fewer than 50 beans in their first two handfuls? How do you know?

Unfold the strip, and show all four numbers. For example:

24	28	23	14

Ask:

Q. Did this pair have more than or fewer than 100 beans in their four handfuls? Explain. About how many beans did they have in their four handfuls? How do you know?

Repeat the activity several times using other pairs' strips.

Explain that partners will explore ways to make 100 by playing a game on the calculator called "Four Steps to 100." The object of the game is to add four numbers on the calculator so that the final total is exactly 100.

Use the overhead calculator and a blank transparency to model the game.

Notes

In this example, students might say:

■ "I know they had more than 50, because 20 and 20 is 40, and 8 and 4 is more than 10, so it's over 50."

■ "Two 25s is 50. 24 is 1 less than 25, but 28 is 3 more. So it's more than 50 beans."

Mathematical Emphasis

Making a reasonable estimate requires gathering and using information.

---

1. Put a number, such as 42, into the overhead calulator and record the number on the blank transparency.

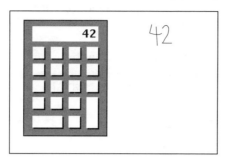

Ask:

Q. What number shall we put in next? Why do you think that is a good choice?

2. Have students suggest a number to add. Record it, and find the total.

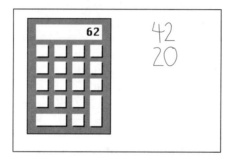

Ask:

Q. We have [62] with only two numbers. What might be a good number for our next turn?

3. Have students suggest another number to add. Repeat Step 2.

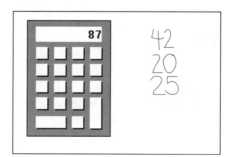

Ask:

Q. We have [87]. What number should we add so that we have exactly 100? How do you know?

4. Have students suggest a final number to add so the total is 100. Record the suggested number and find the total.

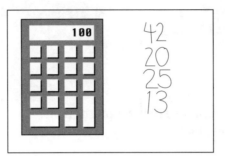

You may want to model the game more than once.

After modeling the game, facilitate a discussion about how partners might work together and fairly share the responsibilities. Ask questions such as:

Social Emphasis
Take responsibility for learning and behavior.

Q. What might you do to make sure you are both involved in playing the game? Why do you think this is important?

Q. If you are unhappy about how you and your partner are working, what might you do? How is that being responsible?

As you observe pairs, ask yourself questions such as:

Q. What strategies do students use to find the four addends? Do they use 50 as a referent? Do they use a guess-and-check approach or some other strategy?

Q. If pairs are referring to the Hundred Chart, how is it helping them to determine the addends?

Observe pairs and ask questions such as:

Q. How are you fairly sharing the work?

Q. How are you making sure you understand each other's ideas?

Q. You have [55] with two numbers. What are two other numbers you might add so that you will land on 100?

In pairs, students use a calculator to find several ways to add four numbers to total 100 and then record the ways.

Have pairs share one of their ways to make 100 with the class. Record the combinations where all can see, and discuss questions such as:

Q. How did you decide what numbers to use?

Q. (Refer to a pair's combination.) **If [Nat] and [Garrett] had added [28] instead of [30] for their last number, what would their final total be? How do you know?**

Have pairs discuss ways they took responsibility for their own learning, helped each other, and fairly shared the calculator and the work. Record any new ideas students have about working together on the "Working Together" chart.

Have pairs explore the Extensions before continuing with the next Lesson.

Mathematical Emphasis

Numbers can be composed and decomposed.

Extensions

For Pairs That Finish Early

- Have pairs play "Four Steps to 100" again, this time adding the rule that they cannot use an addend more than once. If the students have already been playing in this way, have them find several more solutions.

For the Next Day

- If pairs have not explored the Extension For Pairs That Finish Early, have them do so.

- Have pairs play a variation of "Four Steps to 100" in which they find different ways to add [three] numbers to reach a total of 100.

- Continue with the ongoing "Hundreds of Beans" activities, described in the Overview, p. 3.

Two-Hundred Chart Exploration

Students locate numbers, look for patterns, and make observations using the Two-Hundred Chart.

Mathematical Emphasis

In this lesson, students

- Identify patterns.
- Find and compare numbers.
- Informally add and subtract.

Students add to their understanding that

- The same pattern can occur in a variety of settings.
- Number can be composed and decomposed.
- The relative magnitude of numbers can be described.

Social Emphasis

In this lesson, students

- Help each other.
- Share the work.
- Explain their thinking.

Students continue to

- Develop group skills.
- Take responsibility for learning and behavior.

Group Size: 2

Teacher Materials

- Hundred Pocket Chart
- 101–200 Pocket Chart cards
- Transparency of Two-Hundred Chart
- Transparent counter
- Transparency of blank 10 × 10 grid

Student Materials

Each pair needs

- Two-Hundred Chart
- Transparent counter
- Access to a Hundred Chart (from Lesson 3)

Extension Materials

Each pair needs

- Hundred Chart (from Lesson 3)
- Two-Hundred Chart
- Crayons or markers

Notes	**Teacher**	**Students**

Notes column:

Hang the empty Hundred Pocket Chart with only the numeral 101 in the upper left hand corner and the numeral 200 in the lower right hand corner.

Students might call on their knowledge that two 50s or four 25s make 100 to help them think of other combinations of two and four numbers that make 100.

Have students at the overhead projector use the Two-Hundred Chart transparency to explain their thinking.

Teacher column:

Have students discuss the previous two lessons, "One Hundred Beans" and "Four Steps to 100." Ask questions such as:

Q. **What mathematics did we explore in these lessons? What do you know about the number 100 that you didn't know before?**

Q. **What are some ways to make 100 using two numbers? Four numbers? What helps you think of ways to make 100?**

Explain that pairs will build on what they have learned by exploring numbers between 100 and 200 on a Two-Hundred Chart. Refer to the posted Hundred Pocket Chart and, first in pairs, then as a class, discuss questions such as:

Q. **If this Two-Hundred Chart was filled in, what other numbers might be on this chart?**

Q. (Hold up a number such as 110.) **Where do you think [110] might be on this chart? Why?**

Have a pair place [110] in the pocket chart and check for agreement by the class.

Hold up another number, and have students discuss where the number might be in the pocket chart. Have a pair place it in the chart. Repeat the activity with several other numbers.

Distribute a Two-Hundred Chart to each pair, and have pairs discuss and share with the class what they notice about the chart.

After several pairs have shared, provide each pair with a transparent counter. Ask pairs to look at their Two-Hundred Chart and follow your directions:

Q. **Place your counter on the number [132]. How did you find [132]? Did any pair do it a different way? If so, how?**

Notes	Teacher	Students

Teacher

Q. Find the number that is [10] more than [117]. What is that number? How do you know? What number is 20 more? 50 more? Explain.

Students

•• ••

•• ••

Notes

Some pairs may need access to a Hundred Chart.

Teacher

Q. Place your counter on the number that is [30] less than [198]. What is that number? How did you find it on the chart? Explain.

Q. Place your counter on the number that is 100 more than [16]. What is that number? How do you know? What number is [120] more than [16]? Explain.

Mathematical Emphasis

The relative magnitude of numbers can be described.

Teacher

Q. Is [162] greater or less than [150]? Is it closer to [150] or [200]? How do you know?

Explain that pairs will look for patterns on the Two-Hundred Chart and then discuss their discoveries with the class.

Notes

Observe students and note if they make connections between the patterns on the Two-Hundred Chart and the Hundred Chart. Also note how students are including each other and listening to each other's ideas.

Teacher

Observe pairs working and ask questions such as:

Q. What are you discovering about the patterns on the Two-Hundred Chart?

Q. How would you describe a pattern you have found?

Q. In what ways is this chart similar to the Hundred Chart? Different?

Q. How are you making sure to listen to each other's ideas? Does this seem to be fair? Why?

Students

••

In pairs, students explore the Two-Hundred Chart and get ready to report to the class patterns and other interesting discoveries about the chart.

Mathematical Emphasis

The same pattern can occur in a variety of settings.

Teacher

Have several pairs share their discoveries with the class. Discuss questions such as:

Q. What patterns did you discover? How could you describe the pattern? Does that same pattern appear on the Hundred Chart? Explain. What other patterns did you find?

Students

•• ••

•• ••

•• ••

•• ••

Q. **What else did you notice about the numbers on the chart?**

Show the transparency of the blank 10 × 10 Grid, and ask:

Q. (Point to the first empty space on the grid.) **If we were to continue counting on from 200, what number would be in this space? How do you know?**

Q. (Point to the last empty space.) **What number would go here? How do you know?**

Write 201 and 300 in the spaces, point to other empty spaces, and repeat the questions several times. Ask:

Q. **How does knowing the Hundred Chart and Two-Hundred Chart help you answer these questions?**

Help partners reflect on how they worked together by asking questions such as:

Q. **How did you explain your thinking to each other? If you didn't understand your partner's thinking, what did you do? How did that work?**

Q. **How did you come to agreement? Was this ever difficult? If so, how did you solve the problem?**

Q. **How did you fairly share the work? What might you do differently next time?**

Social Emphasis
Take responsibility for learning and behavior.

Extensions

For Pairs That Finish Early

- Have pairs find and color in a pattern that occurs on both the Hundred Chart and the Two-Hundred Chart and find ways the charts are similar.

For the Next Day

- Continue with the ongoing "Hundreds of Beans" activities, described in the Overview, p. 3.

Two-Hundred Chart

101	102	103	104	105	106	107	108	109	110
111	112	113	114	115	116	117	118	119	120
121	122	123	124	125	126	127	128	129	130
131	132	133	134	135	136	137	138	139	140
141	142	143	144	145	146	147	148	149	150
151	152	153	154	155	156	157	158	159	160
161	162	163	164	165	166	167	168	169	170
171	172	173	174	175	176	177	178	179	180
181	182	183	184	185	186	187	188	189	190
191	192	193	194	195	196	197	198	199	200

Find Your Place

Pairs describe the relative magnitude of numbers from the Two-Hundred Chart by comparing them to referents such as 100, 125, 140, 160, and 200.

Mathematical Emphasis

In this lesson, students

- Compare numbers to 100, 125, 140, 160, and 200.

Students add to their understanding that

- The relative magnitude of numbers can be described.

Social Emphasis

In this lesson, students

- Make decisions.
- Move responsibly around the room.

Students continue to

- Develop group skills.
- Take responsibility for learning and behavior.

Group Size: 2

Teacher Materials

- 9″ × 12″ tagboard (see Before the Lesson)
- 5″ × 8″ index card (see Before the Lesson)
- Resealable plastic bag with blank label for each student (see Before the Lesson)
- Copy of "Family Letter" for each student (see Before the Lesson)

Student Materials

Each pair needs

- 5″ × 8″ index card
- Pencil or marker
- Access to a Two-Hundred Chart (see Lesson 7)

Extension Materials

- Pairs' index cards (from the lesson)
- Transparency of blank 10 x 10 grid (from Lesson 7)
- Transparency of the Two-Hundred Chart (from Lesson 7)

- Use 9″ × 12″ sheets of tagboard to make seven signs; six signs labeled "100," "150," "125," "200," "Less than 140," and "More than 160," respectively, and one blank sign. Post the sign labeled "100" and the sign labeled "150" on opposite sides of the room. The other signs will be used later in the lesson.

- Write 137 in large numerals on a 5″ × 8″ index card.

- For each student to take home at the end of this lesson, copy the "Family Letter" and staple it to a small, resealable plastic bag that has a blank adhesive label attached.

Notes

Some students may need a Two-Hundred Chart to help them determine the relationship of a number to other numbers.

Teacher

Introduce the lesson by asking pairs to choose a number on the Two-Hundred Chart and to record their number in large numerals on an index card. Collect the cards.

Show your index card with the number 137 on it and point out the "100" and "150" signs posted on opposite sides of the room. Explain that you want to stand on the side of the room that has the number closest to 137 posted. Ask students to offer suggestions as to where you should stand and to explain their thinking. When the class has agreed, move to the side of the room where "150" is posted.

Randomly distribute one number card per pair. Have pairs look at their number and decide which sign shows a number that is closer to their number. After partners have had a chance to discuss and agree which sign is closer to their number, ask pairs to move to that side of the room.

When pairs have sorted themselves, ask them to take turns showing their number to the other pairs in the group and check to see if everyone in the group agrees that the number belongs with the sign.

Students

•• ••

•• ••

Listing the numbers where all can see will help pairs to discuss the numbers after they return to their seats.

Mathematical Emphasis

The relative magnitude of numbers can be described.

Observe pairs during the activity. Note positive interactions or any problems you may want to discuss.

List pairs' numbers where all can see. For example:

Closer to 100	Closer to 150
110	181
103	199
120	148
	155
	133
	140
	150
	159

Have pairs return to their seats. Referring to the listed numbers, ask questions such as:

Q. **How did you and your partner decide which sign was where your number belonged? Did you agree right away? If not, how did you come to agreement?**

Q. **What do you notice about the other numbers?**

Q. (Point to "Closer to 100.") **Do you agree that all the numbers in this group are closer to 100 than to 150? Why?**

Q. **If we were to list the numbers in order from the least to the greatest, which number would be first? Last? Close to the middle? How do you know?**

Q. **As a class, how did we move around the room in a responsible way? How could we do better?**

Change the signs to "125" and "200." Have partners discuss and decide whether their number is closer to 125 or closer to 200. When they have had a chance to agree, have pairs move to that sign. Ask questions such as:

Q. **What changes do you notice about the numbers in your group?**

Q. (Point to one of the groups.) **Do you think any numbers next to this sign need to be moved? Why?**

Have pairs return to their seats, and ask questions such as:

Q. How do you feel about how we moved around the room this time? What might we do differently?

Change the signs to "Less than 140" and "More than 160." Post the blank sign somewhere between the two. Hold up your number again. Ask pairs to determine where your number would go and to explain their thinking to the class.

Have pairs discuss and decide if their number is less than 140 or more than 160 and move to that side of the room. Explain that if their number does not belong under either sign, they should stand under the blank sign.

When pairs have sorted themselves, ask them to take turns showing their number to other pairs in the group and check to see if everyone agrees that the number belongs with the sign. Ask questions such as:

Q. Does anything surprise you? What?

Some pairs may have numbers from 140 through 160 (for example, 148, 150, 159). These numbers will not fit into either category (less than 140, or more than 160).

Q. What numbers are under the blank sign? Why do these numbers not fit in either of the other categories?

Record the numbers under the blank sign where all can see. For example:

148   159
     150
155   140

Have pairs return to their seats and discuss questions such as:

Students might suggest a category called "More than 139 and less than 161."

Q. What could we call a category in which these numbers would fit? Explain. Could it be called anything else? Why?

Notes	Teacher	Students

Notes

Teacher

Help students reflect on the lesson by asking questions such as:

Q. How did you and your partner decide which sign was where your number belonged? If you disagreed, how did you come to agreement? Did this seem to work? Why? What might you do differently next time?

Q. What helped you move around the room in a way that did not disturb others?

If appropriate, share some of your observations of the positive interactions and problems you noted as pairs worked.

Collect pairs' index cards for use in the Extensions.

Distribute a resealable plastic bag with the attached "Family Letter" to each student. Read the "Family Letter" together. Ask students to write their name on the blank label on the bag. Answer any questions and ask students to bring their collected items to class by the date you wrote in the "Family Letter."

To help students continue to develop their understanding of number relationships and number meaning, have them explore the Extensions.

Students

•• ••

•• ••

For the Next Day

Extensions

- Show a pair's index card from the lesson and have students close their eyes and visualize where the number is on the Two-Hundred Chart. Show the blank 10 x 10 grid transparency on the overhead projector and have students open their eyes. First in pairs, then as a class, discuss where the number is on the chart and in relationship to other numbers (for example, the top half, near the middle, near the bottom, near 150, closer to 200 than to 101). When students have responded, show the Two-Hundred Chart transparency, and have students check their thinking. Repeat the activity several times using other pairs' numbers.

- Randomly distribute the index cards to pairs and have them place the cards in numerical order on the floor, in a chalkboard tray, or on a bulletin board. Provide opportunities for students to explain and verify their thinking.

Dear Parent or Guardian,

Please help your child collect 80–120 small objects. All of these objects should be able to fit into the attached collection bag. For example, a collection might contain 89 bottle caps, 112 buttons, 93 paper clips, or 102 lima beans. We will group, count, compare, and estimate the number of objects in students' collections.

Your child's collection will be returned at the end of the lesson.

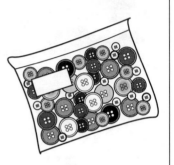

Please have your child bring the collection bag to school by

_____.

Thank you for your help!

Sincerely,

Collections

Students use their collection bags to help them count and estimate 80 to 120 objects.

DAYS AHEAD
5

TRANSITION

Transition Emphasis

In this lesson, students

- Group and count objects.
- Estimate and compute informally.
- Explore relative magnitude.
- Reflect on how they worked together.
- Thank each other.

Students add to their understanding that

- Numbers can be used to describe quantities.
- Quantities of objects can be grouped and counted in a variety of ways.
- Making a reasonable estimate requires gathering and using information.

Social Emphasis

In this lesson, students

- Explain their thinking.
- Share ideas.
- Move responsibly around the room.

Students continue to

- Develop group skills.
- Analyze the effect of behavior on others and on the group work.
- Take responsibility for learning and behavior.

Group Size: 2

Teacher Materials

- 2 collection bags (see Before the Lesson)
- Two 12″ × 18″ construction paper workmats
- Two 5″ × 8″ index cards
- "Things We Know About 100" chart (from Lesson 2)
- "Working Together" chart (from Lesson 1)

Student Materials

Each student needs

- His or her collection bag (see Lesson 8)
- 12″ × 18″ construction paper workmat
- 5″ × 8″ index card

Extension Materials

Each pair needs

- Index cards from the lesson
- Their collection bags
- 5″ × 8″ index card

DAYS AHEAD
5

■ As students bring in their bags of collected items from home (see Lesson 8) have them check to make sure that their name is written clearly on the label. To demonstrate the lesson, you will need two resealable plastic bags, each containing 80–120 similar objects, such as keys, buttons, paperclips, or beads (examples suggested in the lesson are a bag with 112 keys and a bag with 84 buttons). You will also need extra bags for students who are unable to bring objects from home.

■ When all students have their bags of objects, have them share their collections with each other, first in pairs, then as a class.

■ If your students are not familiar with the "Stroll and Stop" strategy (see p. xii), have them practice "Stroll and Stop" prior to the lesson. Discuss how to move around the room in a responsible way.

■ Post the "Things We Know About 100" and "Working Together" charts.

Notes

Teacher

Students

•• ••

•• ••

Introduce the lesson by discussing the mathematics students have been exploring. Explain that pairs will view their collections of 80–120 objects and discuss the different ways the objects can be grouped.

Explain that partners will decide on a way to group the items in each of their collection bags, and then group them. Pairs will then stroll around the room, view other pairs' collections, and discuss the number of objects.

Model the activity by holding up your bag of [buttons] and asking:

Q. How might I group and count these [buttons]?

Using the construction paper as a workmat, follow a student's suggestion for grouping the buttons. For example:

Mathematical Emphasis
Quantities of objects can be grouped and counted in a variety of ways.

•• ••

•• ••

After the buttons are grouped, ask:

Q. About how many buttons are there? Explain.

Together count the buttons in the collection. Record the total in large numerals on an index card.

Repeat the activity with your [key] collection on the second workmat. Discuss questions such as:

Q. Are there more than or fewer than 150 objects altogether in both collections? Why do you think that?

Q. About how many objects are in both collections? Explain.

Explain that pairs will use one bag at a time, decide how to group the objects, then group and count the objects on a workmat and record the number in large numerals on an index card. They will repeat the activity with the other bag on their second workmat.

Before pairs begin, facilitate a discussion about ways they might work together. Ask questions such as:

Q. What have you learned about working together that will help you in this activity?

Q. How might you come to agreement about ways to group and count your items? Why do you think this is fair?

Q. How can you help each other?

Social Emphasis
Develop group skills.

Notes	**Teacher**	**Students**

As you observe students, note how they are working together. Have they grown in their ability to listen to each other? To make decisions together? If so, how?

Observe pairs working and ask questions such as:

Q. **How did you decide to group your objects?**

Q. **How are you sharing the work?**

Q. **About how many objects do you think you have in both bags combined?**

Q. **If you had 100 more objects, how many would you have? How do you know?**

••   In pairs, students

1. Decide how to group the objects in one of their collections.

2. Group the objects on a workmat.

3. Count the objects and record the number in large numerals on an index card.

4. Repeat the activity with the objects in the other collection.

After pairs have finished grouping and counting their objects, collect the index cards for use in Extensions.

Explain that pairs will stroll around the room, view the collections, stop at a pair's collections when you give the "Stop" signal, and discuss the number of objects.

Social Emphasis
Take responsibility for learning and behavior.

As a class, briefly discuss how students might stroll around the room in a responsible way and why it is important to be careful with other pair's collections.

Have pairs stroll around the room to view other pairs' collections. Call "Stop" and have partners discuss the number of items in a nearby collection. Ask one or two of the following questions at each stroll stop:

Observe how students move around the room and discuss other pairs' collections. Ask yourself question such as:

Q. Do students have a sense of the number of objects in the collections?

Q. How do students count the objects? By the displayed groupings? By ones? By another method?

Q. **What do you notice about how the objects in the collections are grouped?**

Q. **What do you notice about the number of objects in the collections?**

Q. **Do you think there are more than [150] objects altogether? Why?**

Q. **[Oleg] and [Ann] say that one collection has [72] objects and the other has [85]. Are there more or fewer than 150 objects altogether? Explain.**

After several strolls and stops, have pairs return to their seats. First in pairs, then as a class, discuss questions such as:

Q. What are some of the activities we participated in during this unit? What did we do with the lima beans? The calculators? What other activities did we do? What numbers did we work with?

Refer to the "Things We Know About 100" chart and review its statements. Ask:

Q. What else have we learned about 100? What can we add to this chart?

Ask pairs to review and discuss the ideas on the "Working Together" chart. Discuss questions such as:

Q. What is one thing that you think is important to do when working with a partner? Why do you think that is important?

Q. Think about how you and your partner worked together at the beginning of this unit, and how you work together now. How have you changed?

Q. Think about how our class has worked together. What do you think we have done well? Where do you think we need to improve?

If appropriate, share your observations of how pairs and the class worked together during the unit. Give partners an opportunity to thank each other.

For Pairs That Finish Early

- Have pairs estimate how many objects they have altogether in their two collections, then find the actual count and record the total on an index card.

For the Next Day

- Have pairs do the activity in Extensions For Pairs That Finish Early, if they have not already done so. As a class, place the cards from Lesson 9 and the cards from the Extension in numerical order on the floor, in a chalk tray, or on a bulletin board. Provide opportunities for students to explain where they think each card should be placed and why.

Mental and Informal Computation

Mathematical Development

This unit helps students develop informal strategies for mentally adding and subtracting with one- and two-digit numbers. Partners play cooperative games with dice, spinners, and a variety of game boards as they help each other to compute mentally. Students are challenged to keep track of ongoing totals as they mentally compute strings of numbers, including multiples of five and ten, and doubled and tripled numbers. Throughout the unit, students devise, use, and explain computation strategies. Students also make estimates, collect and analyze data, and discuss the relative magnitude of numbers.

Social Development

In this unit, students develop their ability to work cooperatively as they play games. Students take responsibility for their learning and behavior as they work, use materials, and make decisions together. Students share the work, listen to others, and explain their thinking. They reflect on ways to help each other and treat each other considerately. Open-ended questions help students examine the effect of behavior on others and on group work. Throughout the unit, students have opportunities to reflect on and write about interactions with their partner.

Students are randomly assigned to pairs that work together throughout the unit.

Mathematical Emphasis

Conceptually, experiences in this unit help students construct their understanding that

- Numbers can be composed and decomposed.

- Problems may have more then one solution and may be solved in a variety of ways.

- Addition and subtraction can be carried out in a variety of ways to arrive at an accurate solution.

- The relative magnitude of numbers can be described.

- Questions about our world can be asked, and data about those questions can be collected, organized, and analyzed.

- Numbers can be used to describe quantities.

Social Emphasis

Socially, experiences in this unit help students to

- Develop group skills.

- Analyze the effect of behavior on others and on the group work.

- Be fair and caring when relating to others.

- Relate the values of fairness, caring, and responsibility to behavior.

Lessons

This unit includes eight mental and informal computation lessons, plus an ongoing mental computation activity. The calendar icon indicates that some preparation is needed or that an experience is suggested for students prior to that lesson.

1. Games!

(page 69)

Team-building lesson in which pairs collect and analyze data about games they like to play.

2. Exactly 100

(page 75)

Mental computation lesson in which pairs use three dice and a 1–120 Chart to add and subtract while trying to reach 100.

3. Cover the Coins

(page 81)

Mental computation lesson in which pairs add money using a spinner and game board.

4. Close to 100

(page 89)

Mental computation lesson in which pairs add and subtract multiples of five and ten as they play a game.

5. Fifty or More

(page 97)

Mental computation lesson in which pairs double, triple, and add numbers as they play a dice game.

6. Take Out Twos

(page 105)

Mental computation lesson in which pairs play a game using three dice, adding the results of five rolls.

7. What's Your Game?

(page 111)

Mental computation lesson in which pairs create a new game based on "Take Out Twos," play it, and share it with the class.

8. Favorite Games

(page 115)

Transition lesson in which students create a class graph showing their favorite games and discuss the data.

"Dice Toss" Activities

These ongoing, teacher-directed, mental computation activities provide opportunities for students to add and subtract the numbers one through six (using regular dice) and add multiples of five and ten (using the teacher-made dice from Lesson 4). The activities are designed to be used frequently over the course of the unit. Begin Activities 1, 2, and 3 after Lesson 2. Begin Activities 4 and 5 after Lesson 4.

Activity 1

Roll three regular dice, and write the numbers rolled where all can see. Have students mentally add the numbers. Ask several students to explain their strategies for adding the numbers.

Activity 2

Roll three regular dice and slowly read aloud the numbers rolled. Have students mentally add the numbers, tell their total to a partner, and, if they disagree, work together to determine the total. Ask several pairs to share their strategies with the class.

Activity 3

Write a number such as 10 where all can see. Roll a die. Ask students to mentally subtract the number rolled, tell the result to a partner, and, if they disagree, work together to determine the total. Ask several pairs to share their strategies with the class.

Activity 4

Roll three of the dice made for Lesson 4 (with the numbers 5, 10, 10, 20, 25, and 50), and write the numbers rolled where all can see. Have students mentally add the numbers. Ask several students to share their strategies with the class.

Activity 5

Roll two of the dice made for Lesson 4, and slowly read aloud the numbers rolled. Have students mentally add the numbers, tell their sum to a partner, and, if they disagree, work together to determine the total. Repeat the activity using three dice.

Materials

The materials needed for the unit are listed below. The first page of each lesson lists the materials specific to that lesson. Blackline masters for transparencies, game boards, score sheets, and record sheets are included at the end of each lesson.

Throughout the unit, you will need an overhead projector, overhead pens, and markers. Students will need access to supplies such as counters, interlocking cubes, paper, and pencils. If possible, each pair should have a container with these supplies available to use at their discretion. Because the focus of the unit is mental computation, students will not need calculators.

Teacher Materials

- Materials for forming pairs (Lesson 1)
- Chart paper (Lessons 1, 2, 3, 4, 5, 6, 8)
- Materials for marking graphs (Lesson 1)
- Transparency of 1–120 Chart (Lesson 2)
- 3 dice (Lessons 2, 5, 6)
- Transparent counters (Lessons 2, 3)
- Transparency of "Cover the Coins" game board (Lesson 3)
- Transparency of "Cover the Coins" spinner (Lesson 3)
- Paper clip (Lesson 3)
- Wooden cubes (Lesson 4)
- Adhesive dots (Lesson 4)
- Transparency of "Close to 100" score sheet (Lesson 4)
- Transparency of "Fifty or More" score sheet (Lesson 5)
- Transparency of "Take Out Twos" score sheet (Lesson 6)

Student Materials

Each pair needs

- 1–120 Chart (Lesson 2)
- 3 dice (Lessons 2, 5, 6)
- Felt or construction paper mat (optional; Lessons 2, 4, 5, 6)
- Transparent counters (Lessons 2, 3)
- "Cover the Coins" game board (Lesson 3)
- "Cover the Coins" spinner (Lesson 3)
- "Close to 100" score sheet(s) (Lesson 4)
- "Fifty or More" score sheet(s) (Lesson 5)
- "Take Out Twos" score sheet(s) (Lesson 6)
- 12″ x 18″ sheet of drawing paper (Lesson 7)
- Self-stick note (Lesson 8)

Each student needs

- "Favorite Games" record sheet (Lesson 8)
- Math Games Folder (Lesson 8)

Extension Materials

Each group of four needs

- Access to games graphs (Lesson 1)
- Sentence strips (Lesson 1)

Each pair needs

- "Close to 100" score sheet(s) (Lesson 4)
- "Fifty or More" score sheet(s) (Lesson 5)
- "Take Out Twos" score sheet(s) (Lesson 6)

Each student needs

- Math Games Folder (Lessons 2, 3, 4, 5, 6, 8)
- "Exactly 100: Extension" record sheet (Lesson 2)
- "Cover the Coins: Extension" record sheet (Lesson 3)
- "Close to 100: Extension" record sheet (Lesson 4)
- "Fifty or More: Extension" record sheet (Lesson 5)
- "Take Out Twos: Extension" record sheet (Lesson 6)

Teaching Hints

- Because this is a unit of cooperative games, it may not be apparent to students that they are exploring important mathematical concepts while participating in the games. Throughout the unit, there are suggested questions to help students become aware of the mathematics. In the Extension For the Next Day for Lessons 2, 3, 4, 5, 6 and 8, students are asked to write about the mathematics in the lesson.

- Several games in this unit require the use of three dice per pair. Dice are available from teacher supply stores and catalogs. Provide time for students to freely explore the dice before they use them in a lesson. Take the time to discuss responsible handling and rolling of the dice. In order to reduce noise, you may want to provide each pair with a felt mat or a piece of heavy construction paper on which to roll the dice.

- In this unit, students are frequently asked to explain their thinking to each other and to the class. To encourage this verbalization, allow enough time for students to think before speaking. Be ready to ask probing questions to help students more fully explain their understanding.

- Extension activities for most of these lessons ask students to reflect on and write about their social interactions and mathematical thinking on a record sheet which contains the rules and materials for the game they learned. For example:

Name _____

Exactly 100

Rules

1. Roll three dice, add the numbers showing, and place a marker on the 1–120 Chart.

2. Roll the dice again and add the sum of the numbers showing to the first total. Move the marker to that total.

3. Continue rolling and adding (subtracting, if necessary) until exactly 100 is reached.

4. If you get close to 100, but have trouble landing on it, you can decide to use one or two dice instead of three.

Materials

❑ 1–120 Chart game board
❑ 3 dice
❑ Transparent counter

---

1. Describe one strategy you used to add or subtract two numbers during the game.

2. What went well while you played "Exactly 100" with your partner? What didn't go very well? What might you do differently next time?

Sally and I took turns rolling the dice. We did not take turns moving the counter. I think we need to take turns moving the counter next time.

Number Power Unit 2, Lesson 2   Exactly 100: Extension Record Sheet   © Developmental Studies Center

---

- Throughout the unit, students are asked to save their record sheets in their own Math Games Folder. The folders will be used at the end of the unit to help students think about the games they played, their mathematical thinking, and how they worked together. After Lesson 8, students will take their folder home in order to play the games and discuss the written reflections with a family member or friend. Provide time for students to share family reactions to the games with the class.

Assessment Techniques

In this unit, students have many opportunities to compose and decompose numbers and use informal strategies to mentally add and subtract. Use the following informal assessment techniques throughout the unit to help you assess students' understandings of these concepts and their ability to apply these understandings. As you observe, also note students' social interactions.

Before each lesson, select some of the suggested open-ended questions to ask your students to explore their mathematical and social understanding, or develop questions of your own. Be ready to probe students' thinking during the lesson by asking follow-up questions that require them to explain further (for example, *How do you know? Say more about that. What do you mean by ___?*) Keep in mind that students' ability to clearly verbalize their thinking does not always match their conceptual understanding. Encourage students to communicate their thinking the best they can, perhaps helping them think about how they would explain their idea to a younger student, or encouraging them to use pictures, diagrams, or manipulatives. Remember that students' ability to verbalize their thinking improves with opportunities to practice over time.

Note that many lessons have an assessment section in the notes column with specific questions you can ask yourself as you observe your students. Whenever possible, record students' responses and compare them over time to assess growth in conceptual understanding. As you observe students throughout the unit, consider using the assessment questions below. Note change in students' conceptual understanding as well as their behavior; for example, *Does the student exhibit confidence in his or her own mathematical thinking? Is he or she able to persevere? Does the student give up easily, suggesting a belief that he or she lacks the ability to solve the problem? If so, does the student experience success and demonstrate more confidence as the unit progresses?*

Observe Individual Students Working

As you observe and listen to students, ask yourself questions such as:

> **Q. What strategies does the student use to mentally add and subtract? Does the student demonstrate flexibility in choosing strategies depending on the numbers being computed?**

For a problem like 25 + 12 = ___, students may use strategies such as:

- **decomposing numbers** (students may decompose the 12 into 10 and 2 and think "25 + 10 = 35, 35 + 2 = 37," or decompose the 12 into 5 and 7 and think "25 + 5 = 30, 30 + 7 = 37.");

- **using a Hundred Chart** ("go down one row on the chart and two spaces to the right");

- **adding tens and ones separately** ("20 + 10 = 30, 5 + 2 = 7, 30 + 7 = 37.");

- simply **counting** by ones, twos, fives, tens, etc. ("25, 26, 27, 28...37," or "25, 30, 35, 36, 37").

To add a series of numbers, students may look first for addends that are compatible with each other and therefore easy to add, such as doubles or combinations that equal ten. Students demonstrate flexibility by being able to call on different strategies that are appropriate for the numbers they are using.

> **Q. Does the student have a sense that the relative magnitude of a number is based on its relationship to other numbers?**

Students who have a sense of the relative magnitude of 56, for example, can recognize that 56 is closer to 60 than to 50, but closer to 50 than to 100. They can estimate that 56 added to a number like 64 would result in a sum greater than 100, as both numbers are greater than 50. Concepts of relative magnitude are often developed informally through manipulating quantities and through conversations about numbers. These understandings are crucial to developing number sense and an ability to reason with numbers accurately.

Reflect on Your Role as Teacher

As you reflect on your role in each lesson, consider the following questions:

Q. Did I allow time for students to reason through and explain their own strategies, or did I inadvertently impose my thinking? Did I ask open-ended questions? Did I encourage a variety of responses? How did I handle the unexpected?

Q. When I asked follow-up questions to probe students' thinking, were students able to expand on and further clarify their thinking, or did they become confused? Was this caused by my choice of questions or by students' lack of understanding or confidence?

Q. What part of the lesson went well? Why? What part would I change the next time? Why?

Q. What additional experiences would enhance students' understanding?

Student Writing

Throughout this unit, students are asked to reflect on and write about their social interactions and mathematical thinking on record sheets they keep in a Math Games Folder. Students might write about what helped them work together or how they solved a problem. They might describe a strategy they used to mentally compute two numbers. To stimulate their thinking, give students time to discuss the topic before asking them to write.

Games!

Students get to know more about each other and their class as they graph and interpret data about the games they like to play.

DAYS AHEAD 2

TEAM BUILDER

Team Builder Emphasis

In this lesson, students

■ Get to know each other.
■ Make predictions.
■ Graph and interpret data.
■ Make statements summarizing data.

Students add to their understanding that

■ Questions about our world can be asked, and data about those questions can be collected, organized, and analyzed.

Social Emphasis

In this lesson, students

■ Make decisions.
■ Move responsibly around the room.

Students continue to

■ Develop group skills.
■ Be fair and caring when relating to others.
■ Analyze the effect of behavior on others and on the group work.

Group Size: 2

Teacher Materials

■ Materials for forming pairs (see Before the Lesson)
■ Games graphs (see Before the Lesson)
■ Materials for marking graphs (see Before the Lesson)

Extension Materials

Each group of four needs

■ Access to games graphs (from the lesson)
■ Sentence strips and a pencil

I like to play some games indoors and some games outdoors.

Me too! Why don't we write two X's where the circles overlap?

- Decide how you will form pairs to work together during the unit (see Forming Groups, p. xiii, for random-grouping suggestions). Prepare any materials needed.

- Make each of the following graphs on a large sheet of paper.

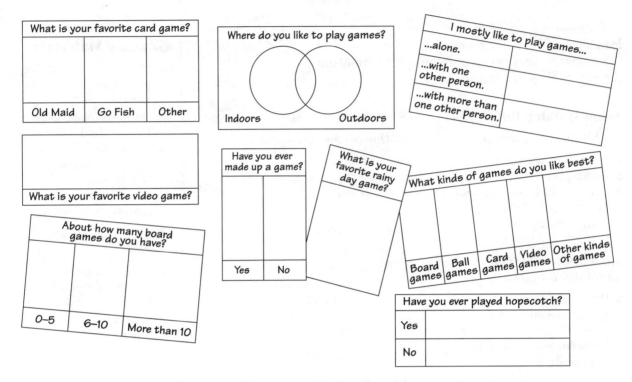

- Gather appropriate materials needed to mark the graphs. You may wish to include a variety of materials, such as self-adhesive dots, color markers, and so on.

- If your students are not familiar with the "Strolling" strategy, have them practice "Strolling" prior to the lesson (see p. xii for suggestions). Discuss how students might move around the room in a responsible way.

Notes	Teacher	Students

Notes

Be sure that partners know each other's names.

A cooperative strategy such as "Turn to Your Partner" (see p. xii) can provide opportunities for all students to be involved in the discussion.

Students might mention:

- Using addition to keep score in team games, video games, and card games.
- Counting money in board games.
- Keeping track of time remaining in sports games.

By marking each other's responses on the graphs, partners have an opportunity to practice their listening skills.

Teacher

Form pairs using the activity you have chosen. Explain that pairs will work together during this unit as the class learns about addition and subtraction by playing many different games. Explain that partners will help each other to add and subtract. First in pairs, then as a class, discuss questions such as:

Q. **What kinds of games do you like to play? Why do you like that kind of game? What are some other kinds of games?**

Q. **What kinds of games use numbers in them? How are numbers used in these games? Do you ever need to use math in these games? When? What kind of math?**

Q. **What is your favorite indoor game? Why do you like it? Outdoor game?**

Q. **What are some board games you have played? Card games? How are board games and card games alike? How are they different?**

Explain that students will have an opportunity to find out the kinds of games their partners like by marking several graphs about games together.

Show and read the title of each graph to the class. Discuss possible ways to answer each question and to mark the answers on the graphs. Place the graphs on students' desks throughout the room in order to provide a flat surface for easy marking.

Model the activity with several students as your partner. With each partner, stroll around the room to several graphs and have your partner mark your responses on the graphs, as you mark his or her responses. Ask questions such as:

Q. **What might be a way to decide on which graph to mark first?**

Students

•• ••

•• ••

Notes	Teacher	Students

Social Emphasis
Be fair and caring when relating to others.

Q. **What might you do if you go to a graph where other students are? How can you be fair to them?**

Q. **How can you help your partner know how to mark your response on the graph?**

Q. **How can you move around the room in a responsible way?**

Have pairs stroll around the room and mark the graphs.

•• ••

•• ••

As you observe students marking the graphs, ask yourself questions such as:

Q. Do students understand what each graph is asking and how to mark it?

Q. Are students moving around the room in a responsible way? Are they treating each other in a fair and caring manner? How? If not, what might you ask students to help them think about other ways to work?

Observe pairs and ask questions such as:

Q. **What are you finding out about your partner? What games do you both like? Does that surprise you?**

Q. **At this point, about how many students have marked** [Old Maid] **as their favorite card game? How do you know? Do you think** [Old Maid] **will be marked more times or fewer times than** [Go Fish]**?**

Q. **What do the data collected at this point on the** ["Have you ever played hopscotch?"] **graph tell us about our class?**

••

In pairs, students stroll around the room and mark each graph.

Mathematical Emphasis
Questions about our world can be asked, and data about those questions can be collected, organized, and analyzed.

After students have marked each graph, post the "What kind of games do you like best?" graph. First in pairs, then as a class, discuss the data recorded on the graph. Ask questions such as:

Q. **What are some things the data on this graph tell you? How do you know?**

Q. **What surprises you about the data on this graph? Why?**

•• ••

•• ••

Help students reflect on the lesson by asking questions such as:

Q. **What new things did you learn about your partner? Classmates?**

Q. **How did "strolling" around the class-room in a responsible way help our class work well together? How might we act even more responsibly next time?**

Save the "Have you ever made up a game?" graph for use in Lesson 2. Save the other graphs for use in Extensions For the Next Day. Have students do the Extensions For the Next Day before going on to the next lesson.

Extensions

For Pairs That Finish Early

■ Have each pair brainstorm and record a list of games that both part-ners like and then circle the games that have mathematics in them. Ask partners to make sure they agree on the games they list and circle. Provide time later for pairs to share with the class the games they cir-cled and the mathematics in them.

For the Next Day

■ Have each pair join another pair to make groups of four. Ask each group to choose one of the graphs from this lesson, and discuss and record on sentence strips several statements about the data. Post the graphs and statements. After groups "stroll" around the classroom to view the graphs and read the statements, facilitate a class discussion about the statements for each graph.

Exactly 100

P̲airs use a 1–120 Chart to play a game in which they add and subtract the sum of three dice in order to reach exactly 100.

Mathematical Emphasis

In this lesson, students

- Mentally add and subtract.
- Compose and decompose numbers.

Students add to their understanding that

- Numbers can be composed and decomposed.
- Addition and subtraction can be carried out in a variety of ways to arrive at an accurate solution.
- Problems may have more than one solution and may be solved in a variety of ways.

Social Emphasis

In this lesson, students

- Reach agreement.
- Make decisions.
- Use materials responsibly.
- Explain their thinking.

Students continue to

- Develop group skills.
- Analyze the effect of behavior on others and on the group work.

Group Size: 2

Teacher Materials

- "Have you ever made up a game?" graph (from Lesson 1)
- Transparency of 1–120 Chart (from Unit 1, Lesson 4; see Before the Lesson)
- "Exactly 100" rules chart (see Before the Lesson)
- 3 dice
- Transparent counter

Student Materials

Each pair needs

- 1–120 Chart (from Unit 1, Lesson 4)
- 3 dice and mat (see Before the Lesson)
- Transparent counter

Extension Materials

Each pair needs

- "Exactly 100" game materials

Each student needs

- Math Games Folder (see Before the Lesson)
- "Exactly 100: Extension" record sheet

■ Students use a 1–120 Chart as a game board in this lesson. The 1–120 Chart allows students to go over or under 100 as they target 100 in this game. Students were introduced to the 1–120 Chart in Unit 1, Lesson 4, when they played "One Hundred or More." Students will play a similar but more challenging game with the 1–120 Chart in this lesson. You may want to provide opportunities for students to review the chart and compare it to a Hundred Chart before playing the game. Ask questions such as:

Q. **What number is 10 more than** [84]? **How do you know? 20 more? How do you know?**

Q. **What number is 10 less than** [113]? **How do you know?**

Q. **How is this chart** [similar to/different from] **the Hundred Chart?**

■ Make a large "Exactly 100" rules chart, such as the one below, and post.

Exactly 100

1. Roll three dice, add the numbers showing, and place a marker on the 1–120 Chart.

2. Roll the dice again and add the sum of the first number showing to the first total. Move the marker to that total.

3. Continue rolling and adding (subtracting, if necessary) until exactly 100 is reached.

4. If you get close to 100, but have trouble landing on it, you can decide to use one or two dice instead of three.

■ Noise from rolling dice can be diminished by having students roll their dice on a felt mat or a piece of construction paper.

■ Provide each student with a file folder to use as a Math Game Folder (see Overview, p. 65). Students will save their written work for the unit in this folder.

■ Post the "Have you ever made up a game?" graph from Lesson 1.

Notes

A cooperative structure such as "Turn to Your Partner" (see p. xii) can provide opportunities for all students to be involved in the discussion.

The "Exactly 100" game was adapted from *Young Children Continue to Reinvent Arithmetic – 2nd Grade: Implications of Piaget's Theory*, by Constance Kamii with Linda Leslie Joseph (New York: Teachers' College Press, 1989).

If students have not had experience using dice, you may want to ask several students to model using them in a quiet and responsible way.

Ask students to verbalize their strategies when adding a new sum to a previous total to encourage the development of computation strategies. For example, students might say:

- "To add 32 and 13, I did 22 plus 10 is 32 and moved the counter down one row, then I added 3. 32...33, 34, 35."
- "I checked the answer by counting up 13 from 22. 22, 23, 24...35."

Teacher

Introduce the lesson by having students refer to the "Have you ever made up a game?" graph. Ask questions such as:

Q. **What are some things the data on this graph tell you?**

Q. **Do the data surprise you?**

Q. **What kinds of games have you created?**

Explain that pairs will play a game called "Exactly 100," which is similar to one created by a group of second grade students in Alabama. Explain that in this game pairs will work together to practice mentally adding and subtracting the numbers shown on three dice until they reach 100 exactly, and that a 1–120 Chart will be used as a game board.

Show the 1–120 Chart transparency, and model the game with a student as your partner.

1. Roll three dice and together mentally add the numbers shown, discussing your strategy with your partner. When you agree on the total, place a transparent counter on the number on the game board.

2. Have your partner roll the dice and together mentally add the numbers shown. When you agree on the sum, add it to the previous total, explaining your strategies. Make sure you agree on the new total before moving your marker.

3. Continue taking turns. As you get close to or just over 100, discuss whether you will need to add or subtract to land on 100 and explain your reasoning.

4. If you get close to 100, but have trouble landing on it, you may decide to use one or two dice instead of all three.

Students

•• ••

•• ••

Notes	Teacher	Students

Have students discuss what they noticed about how you and your partner worked together. Ask questions such as:

•• ••

•• ••

Social Emphasis
Analyze the effect of behavior on others and on the group work.

Q. **What helped us work together well? What might you suggest to help us work together even better?**

Q. **How did we use the materials in a responsible way? How did that help our work?**

Model the game again by having pairs play the game as you roll the dice for the class. Ask questions such as:

Mathematical Emphasis
Addition and subtraction can be carried out in a variety of ways to arrive at an accurate solution.

Q. **We are on [58] and we rolled [11]. Where will you and your partner move the marker? How did you add the numbers? Explain.**

Q. **We are on [80]. Can we reach exactly 100? How do you know?**

Q. **(Roll the dice.) Should we add or subtract? Why? If we subtract, where will we put the marker? How do you know? If we add, where will we put the marker? Explain.**

Q. **We have gotten close to 100 several times but haven't landed on exactly 100 yet. Should we try rolling two dice instead of three? How might that help us?**

Refer to the posted "Exactly 100" rules chart, and review the rules. Have pairs play "Exactly 100."

Observe how students interact. Note positive interactions or problems you might want to discuss when the class reflects on the lesson.

Observe pairs and ask questions such as:

Q. **You are on [32]. What number would you need to roll in order to land on [43]? How do you know?**

Q. **Why did you subtract?**

Q. **How are you sharing the materials and the work?**

••

In pairs, students play "Exactly 100."

Notes	**Teacher**	**Students**

Teacher

After all pairs have played the game at least one time, ask questions such as:

Q. **What did you learn about the number 100 while playing the game? Explain.**

Q. **When your score got close to 100, how did you decide whether to add or to subtract?**

Q. **Did any pair decide to use one or two dice instead of all three? Why did you make that decision?**

Q. **What did you find hard about the game? Easy? Explain.**

Q. **What did you find hard about playing the game together? What did you find easy?**

Q. **What did you learn about playing a game together that will help you play together next time?**

If appropriate, share some of your observations of the positive interactions and the problems you noted as students worked.

Save the "Exactly 100" rules chart for use in Lesson 8.

To provide students with an opportunity to explain their thinking in writing and to explore their social interactions, have students explore Extensions For the Next Day before going on to the next lesson.

Mathematical Emphasis

Problems may have more than one solution and may be solved in a variety of ways.

Extensions

For Pairs That Finish Early

- Have pairs play "Exactly 100" again.

For the Next Day

- Have pairs play "Exactly 100" again. Then, as a class, read and discuss the questions on the bottom half of the "Exactly 100" record sheet. Have each student respond to the questions in writing. Provide time for pairs to share their responses with each other, and then ask several pairs to share with the class. Have students place their record sheet in their Math Games Folder.

- Begin the ongoing "Dice Toss" Activities 1–3 described in the Overview, p. 63.

Exactly 100

Rules

1. Roll three dice, add the numbers showing, and place a marker on the 1–120 Chart.

2. Roll the dice again and add the sum of the numbers showing to the first total. Move the marker to that total.

3. Continue rolling and adding (subtracting, if necessary) until exactly 100 is reached.

4. If you get close to 100, but have trouble landing on it, you can decide to use one or two dice instead of three.

Materials

❏ 1–120 Chart game board

❏ 3 dice

❏ Transparent counter

1. Describe one strategy you used to add or subtract two numbers during the game.

2. What went well while you played "Exactly 100" with your partner? What didn't go very well? What might you do differently next time?

Cover the Coins

Pairs mentally compute with different amounts of money as they play a game with spinners and a game board.

DAYS AHEAD
1

Mathematical Emphasis

In this lesson, students

- Mentally add and subtract using multiples of five and ten.

Students add to their understanding that

- Numbers can be composed and decomposed.
- Problems may have more than one solution and may be solved in a variety of ways.
- Addition and subtraction can be carried out in a variety of ways to arrive at an accurate solution.

Social Emphasis

In this lesson, students

- Share the work.
- Share materials.
- Make decisions.
- Explain their thinking.

Students continue to

- Develop group skills.
- Relate the values of fairness, caring, and responsibility to behavior.

Group Size: 2

Teacher Materials

- "Cover the Coins" rules chart (see Before the Lesson)
- Transparencies of "Cover the Coins" game board and spinner
- Paper clip
- Transparent counters
- Paper and a pencil

Student Materials

Each pair needs

- "Cover the Coins" game board and spinner (see Before the Lesson)
- Paper clip
- Transparent counters
- Paper and a pencil

Extension Materials

Each pair needs

- "Cover the Coins" game materials

Each student needs

- "Cover the Coins: Extension" record sheet
- Math Games Folder

We spun 35 cents. What coins should we cover?

We could cover three 10 cent coins and one 5 cent coin, or even seven 5 cent coins.

Or we could cover the other quarter and one of the 10 cent coins.

■ Copy the "Cover the Coins" Spinners blackline master and cut apart so you have one spinner for each pair. Students can use a pencil and paper clip as a spinner by anchoring the paper clip with the pencil and spinning the paper clip (see diagram below). You may choose to use plastic spinner arrows instead (available at teacher supply centers).

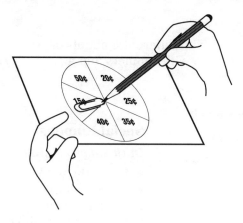

■ If students have not previously worked with spinners, allow time for free exploration before this lesson.

■ Before playing "Cover the Coins," you may want to provide opportunities for students to explore real, paper, or plastic coins and to practice writing out amounts larger than $1.00 (for example, $1.15, $1.30, $1.45). As pairs explore, ask questions such as:

Q. What coins might you use to make [$1.60]? How might you write [$1.60]?

■ Make a large "Cover the Coins" rules chart, such as the one below, and post.

Cover the Coins

1. Spin the spinner to find the amount of money to be covered.

2. Cover the coins.

3. Continue to spin and cover the coins for a total of five spins or until all the coins are covered.

4. Find the total amount of money covered and record it.

| **Notes** | **Teacher** | **Students** |

Introduce the lesson by reviewing the game "Exactly 100" from the previous lesson. Ask:

••   ••

••   ••

Q. When you played "Exactly 100," what helped you and your partner work well together?

Q. How did we use numbers in "Exactly 100"? What did you need to subtract?

Explain that pairs will play another game called "Cover the Coins" and that they will continue to practice adding and subtracting numbers in their minds. As a class, read and discuss the rules of the game.

Show the "Cover the Coins" transparency, and ask questions such as:

Mathematical Emphasis

Numbers can be composed and decomposed.

Q. What coins could be covered if you spin [20¢]? Is there another way to cover [20¢]? Explain.

Q. If you spin [35¢], how many ways could the coins be covered? How do you know?

Model the game with a student as your partner:

1. Spin the spinner.

2. With your partner, decide which coins to cover with the transparent counters.

3. Taking turns with your partner, continue to spin, decide, and cover the coins for a total of five spins or until all the coins are covered.

4. Find the total of the covered coins, and record the total on a sheet of paper.

Model the game again by having pairs play the game as you spin the spinner for the class. As pairs play, ask questions such as:

Q. [Narek] and [Gillian] covered [one nickel and one dime]. Is there another way to cover [15¢]?

Notes	**Teacher**	**Students**
	After five spins, have several pairs share their results and explain how they would find the total amount covered.	●● ●● ●● ●●
Social Emphasis Relate the values of fairness, caring, and responsibility to behavior.	First in pairs, then as a class, discuss what might help pairs work together. Ask questions such as: Q. **How will you make decisions about which coins to cover? Why do you think this is a fair and responsible way?** Q. **How will you share the work and the materials?** Review the rules, and have pairs play the game.	

As you observe students, ask yourself questions such as: Q. How are students working together? Are they sharing the work? Materials? Are they asking for their partner's thinking? Q. Do students show flexibility in their thinking? Are they able to think of more than one way to cover the coins? Q. How do students find the total after five spins?	**O**bserve pairs and ask questions such as: Q. **Is there another way to cover [40¢]? Explain.** Q. **What amount do you have covered on your game board now? How do you know? How much more would you need to cover to make [$1.00]?** Q. **How are you both participating in the game? How are you sharing the work and the materials?**	●● In pairs, students play "Cover the Coins."

Provide sufficient time for pairs to explore these questions. **A** cooperative strategy such as "Think, Pair, Share" (see p. xii) can provide opportunities for all students to reflect on a problem before discussing their thinking.	**A**fter pairs have played the game a few times, ask several pairs to report one of their totals. List the totals where all can see. Ask questions such as: Q. (Point to one of the numbers.) **This pair had a total of [$1.20]. What coins might they have covered? Is there another way they might have covered [$1.20]?**	●● ●● ●● ●●

Mathematical Emphasis

Problems may have more than one solution and may be soved in a variety of ways.

•• ••

•• ••

Q. (Point to another number.) **This pair had a total of [$1.45]. How much more would they need to have [$2.00]? How do you know?**

Q. **Is there a total that is close to [$1.50]? How do you know? Close to [$2.00]? Explain.**

Q. **If [$1.60] and [$1.75] are added together, would the total be more than or less than [$3.00]? How do you know?**

Q. **How could playing a game like "Cover the Coins" help you when using real money?**

Help students reflect on the lesson by having partners discuss what they did that helped them work together and any problems they had. If pairs wish to do so, have them share some of their problems and have the class discuss some possible solutions.

Save the "Cover the Coins" rules chart for use in Lesson 8.

To provide students with further opportunities to explain their thinking in writing and to explore their social interactions, have them explore the Extensions For the Next Day before going on to the next lesson.

Extensions

For Pairs That Finish Early

■ Have pairs play "Cover the Coins" again.

For the Next Day

■ Have pairs play "Cover the Coins" again. Then, as a class read and discuss the questions on the "Cover the Coins" record sheet. Have each student respond to the questions in writing. Provide time for pairs to share their responses with each other, and then ask several pairs to share with the class. Have students place the record sheet in their Math Games Folder.

■ Continue with the ongoing "Dice Toss" Activities 1–3 described in the Overview, p. 63.

Cover the Coins

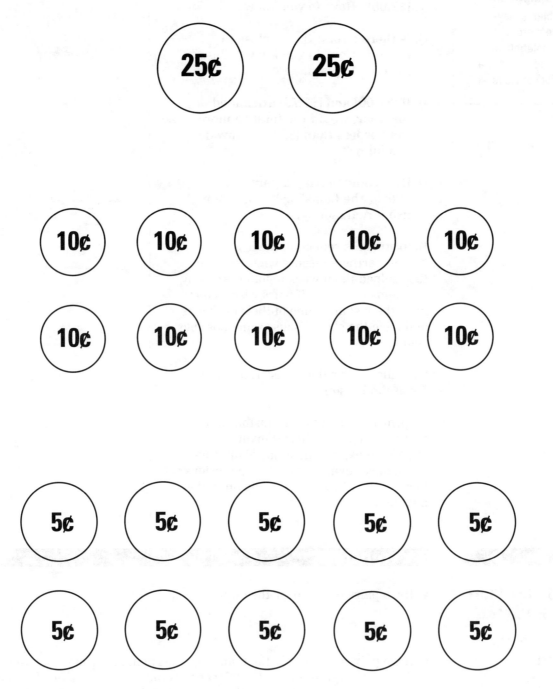

Cover the Coins Spinners

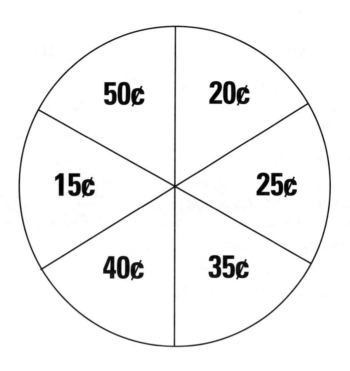

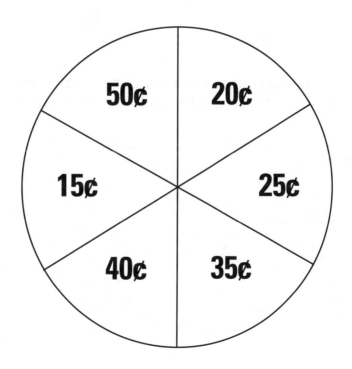

Cover the Coins

Rules

1. Spin the spinner to find the amount of money to be covered.
2. Cover the coins.
3. Continue to spin and cover the coins for a total of five spins or until all the coins are covered.
4. Find the total amount of money covered and record it.

Materials

- ❏ "Cover the Coins" game board
- ❏ "Cover the Coins" spinner
- ❏ Paper clip
- ❏ Transparent counters
- ❏ Paper and a pencil

1. Describe how you added to find the total amount of money covered on your record sheet.

2. How did you and your partner share the work when you played "Cover the Coins"? Do you feel that was fair? Why?

Close to 100

Students play a game in which they mentally add and subtract multiples of five and ten while trying to reach 100.

Mathematical Emphasis

In this lesson, students

- Mentally add and subtract multiples of five and ten.

Students add to their understanding that

- Numbers can be composed and decomposed.
- Problems may have more than one solution and may be solved in a variety of ways.

Social Emphasis

In this lesson, students

- Share the work.
- Use materials responsibly.
- Make decisions.
- Reach agreement.

Students continue to

- Develop group skills.
- Relate the values of fairness, caring, and responsibility to behavior.

Group Size: 2

Teacher Materials

- "Close to 100" rules chart (see Before the Lesson)
- Die made with wooden cubes and adhesive dots (see Before the Lesson)
- Transparency of "Close to 100" score sheet and a marker

Student Materials

Each pair needs

- Die and mat (see Before the Lesson)
- "Close to 100" score sheet(s)

Extension Materials

Each pair needs

- "Close to 100" game materials, including "Close to 100" score sheet(s)

Each student needs

- "Close to 100: Extension" record sheet
- Math Games Folder

■ Make a die for each pair with the following numbers on the faces: 5, 10, 10, 20, 25, 50. To make the dice, write the numbers on adhesive dots and place the dots on wooden cubes.

■ Noise from rolling dice can be diminished by having students roll their die on a felt mat or piece of construction paper.

■ Make a "Close to 100" rules chart, such as the one below, and post.

Close to 100

1. Roll the die and record the number.

2. Roll the die again. Add the number to the number rolled previously and record the total.

3. Continue to roll for a total of ten rolls, deciding when to add or subtract to get close to 100 without going over.

4. After the last roll, find out how far away your total is from 100, and record the answer.

Notes

Mathematical Emphasis

Numbers can be composed and decomposed.

Teacher

First in pairs, then as a class, discuss the following question:

Q. **What numbers can you put together to make 100?**

As students respond, list the combinations where all can see. Ask questions such as:

Q. **What do you notice about the combinations that are listed?**

Q. **Do you think we have listed all the possible combinations that make 100? Why do you think that?**

Explain that pairs will play a new game called "Close to 100" in which they will practice mentally adding and subtracting numbers to get close to 100. Show a sample die and explain that it has 5, 10, 10, 20, 25, and 50 on its faces.

Students

●● ●●

●● ●●

Refer to the "Close to 100" rules chart and discuss the rules. Use the "Close to 100" transparency and a die to model the game with a student as your partner.

Roll	Total
+ 10	10

1. Roll the die. Read aloud the number rolled and record it on the transparency in the "Roll" column and in the "Total" column.

2. Have your partner roll the die, read aloud the number rolled, and record the number in the "Roll" column. With your partner, decide whether to add or subtract the number rolled to the previous total and record a "+" or "–" sign. Agree on the sum or difference and record the results in the "Total" column.

3. Taking turns with your partner, continue to roll the die for a total of ten rolls, each time deciding whether to add or subtract the number rolled.

Roll	Total
+10	10
+20	30
+20	50
+10	60
-50	10
+50	60
-50	10
+5	15
+10	25
+20	45

We need <u>55</u> to make 100.

4. After the tenth roll, find the difference between the total and 100, and record this on the bottom of the record sheet.

Ask pairs to discuss what they noticed about how you and your partner played the game responsibly. Ask questions such as:

Q. What did my partner and I do that helped us work well together?

Q. What might help you and your partner work well together?

Model the game again by having pairs play the game as you roll the die for the class. Discuss questions such as:

Be aware that it is not unusual in this game for the last total to be fairly far away from 100.

Q. Did you decide to add or subtract the number rolled? Why? What is your result? How do you know?

Q. Did someone make a different decision? What is your result?

Notes	Teacher	Students

Q. [Homer] **and** [Serina] **have** [65]. **How many more do they need to have 100? How do you know? Does any pair have a number closer to 100 than** [65]**?**

•• ••

•• ••

After ten rolls of the die, discuss pairs' results and the different strategies they used to play the game.

Refer to the posted chart, review the game rules, and have pairs play the game.

As you observe pairs, ask yourself questions such as:

Q. How are pairs deciding to add or subtract?

Q. What strategies are students using to subtract? Do they count up and back using fives and tens or do they count only by ones?

Q. Are both students actively involved in the game?

Observe pairs and ask questions such as:

Q. **Are you going to add or subtract? Why?**

Q. **How many more do you need to make 100? Can you make 100 in** [two] **more rolls? How?**

Q. **How are you sharing the work? Do you think this is fair? Why?**

••

In pairs, students play "Close to 100."

After all pairs have played at least one round of the game, ask questions such as:

•• ••

•• ••

Q. **Did any pair get a number close to 100? How many points would you need to have 100? How do you know?**

Mathematical Emphasis

Problems may have more than one solution and may be solved in a variety of ways.

Q. **If you have** [55] **and you roll** [25]**, what sum or difference could you have? How do you know?**

Q. **If you were to play the game again, would you use a different strategy? Explain.**

Q. **What did you learn about adding and subtracting numbers while playing "Close to 100?"**

Notes	Teacher	Students

Social Emphasis
Relate the values of fairness, caring, and responsibility to behavior.

Help students reflect on the lesson by asking questions such as:

Q. How did you and your partner make decisions about whether to add or subtract? Was that fair? Why?

Q. How did you and your partner help each other? What might you do differently the next time?

Save the "Close to 100" rules chart for use in Lesson 8.

To provide students further opportunities to reflect on the mathematics they explored while playing "Close to 100," have them explore the Extensions For the Next Day before going on to the next lesson.

•• ••

•• ••

Extensions

For Pairs That Finish Early

- Have pairs play "Close to 100" again.

For the Next Day

- Have pairs play "Close to 100" again. Then, as a class, read and discuss the questions on the "Close to 100" record sheet. Have each student respond to the questions in writing. Provide time for pairs to share their responses with each other, and then ask several pairs to share with the class. Have students place the record sheet in their Math Games Folder.

- Continue with the ongoing "Dice Toss" Activities 1–3, and add Activities 4–5, as described in the Overview, p. 63.

Close to 100
Score Sheet

Roll	Total

We need _____ to make 100.

Close to 100

Rules

1. Roll the die and record the number.

2. Roll the die again. Add the number to the number rolled previously and record the total.

3. Continue to roll for a total of ten rolls, deciding when to add or subtract to get close to 100 without going over.

4. After the last roll, find out how far away your total is from 100, and record the answer.

Materials

❏ "Close to 100" record sheet

❏ Die labeled 5, 10, 10, 20, 25, 50

❏ Pencil

1. When you played the game "Close to 100," what strategies did you use to decide whether to add or to subtract the number rolled?

2. Describe the strategy you used to figure out how far away your total was from 100.

Fifty or More

Students play a dice game in which they mentally add doubles and triples to a sum of at least 50.

Mathematical Emphasis

In this lesson, students

- Mentally add and subtract.
- Estimate differences and sums.

Students add to their understanding that

- Numbers can be composed and decomposed.
- Addition and subtraction can be carried out in a variety of ways to arrive at an accurate solution.
- The relative magnitude of numbers can be described.

Social Emphasis

In this lesson, students

- Share materials.
- Help each other.
- Explain their thinking.
- Explore ways to be considerate of each other.

Students continue to

- Develop group skills.
- Explore ways to be fair and caring when relating to others.

Group Size: 2

Teacher Materials

- "Fifty or More" rules chart (see Before the Lesson)
- 3 dice
- Transparency of "Fifty or More" score sheet and a marker

Student Materials

Each pair needs

- 3 dice and mat
- "Fifty or More" score sheet(s)

Extension Materials

Each pair needs

- "Fifty or More" game materials including "Fifty or More" score sheet(s)

Each student needs

- "Fifty or More: Extension" record sheet
- Math Games Folder

■ Make a "Fifty or More" rules chart, such as the one below, and post.

Fifty or More

1. Roll 3 dice.

2. If you roll double or triple 1s, 2s, 4s, or 5s, add the numbers that make the double or triple and record the total on the "Fifty or More" score sheet.

3. If you roll double or triple 3s, subtract all your points and go back to 0.

4. If you roll double 6s, add 25 points. If you roll triple 6s, add 50 points.

5. Continue to roll and record until you reach a total of 50 or more points.

Notes

If students have difficulty figuring out what a roll is worth, you might draw a diagram like the one below and ask students to tell you what each roll would be worth.

0 points
(No double or triple)

8 points
(Double 4s)

15 points
(Triple 5s)

Subtract all points and go back to 0!
(Double 3s)

25 points
(Double 6s)

50 points
(Triple 6s)

Teacher

Introduce the lesson by having pairs review the games they played and the mathematics they used in the previous lessons.

Explain that pairs will use three dice to play a game called "Fifty or More," in which they will mentally add doubles and triples and compute to a sum of at least 50. Refer to the "Fifty or More" rules chart and explain each rule. Ask questions such as:

Q. What is meant by rolling doubles? Triples?

Q. If I roll double fours, how many points would I add? How do you know? Triple fours?

Roll three dice several times, recording the numbers rolled where all can see. After each roll ask:

Q. Are there any doubles? Triples? How many points would we add on this roll? How do you know?

Model playing the game with a student as your partner.

Students

●● ●●

●● ●●

•• ••

•• ••

1. Roll three dice and tell the class the numbers rolled. Mentally add any doubles or triples, and record the sum on the "Fifty or More" score sheet transparency.

2. Have your partner roll the dice, tell the class the numbers rolled, and mentally add any doubles and triples. Have your partner record the sum and new total on the "Fifty or More" score sheet.

3. Continue to take turns with your partner, rolling and adding until the total score is 50 or more points. Long games may need to be continued on a separate sheet of paper.

Have pairs play one game with you rolling the dice for the class. Stop periodically to review the rules and ask questions such as:

Students might say:

■ "We need 24 more. I added 2 tens to 26 and got 46. Then I added four more to make 50."

■ "I added four to 26 to get 30. Then I added 20 more, so it is 24."

■ "If we had 25, we would need 25 more to make 50. But we have 26, so we need 1 less, that's 24."

Q. We have [26]. How many more do we need to have 50? How do you know?

Q. If we add [15] to [37], will we have more than 50 or less than 50? How do you know?

Have pairs discuss ways they can play the game so that both partners are involved in sharing the work and mentally adding the numbers. Ask questions such as:

Q. You and your partner may need different amounts of time to add mentally. What can you do to be considerate of your partner?

Q. If your partner needs help, how can you help him or her without just telling the answer? What can you do to help your partner be considerate of you? Why is that important?

Refer to the posted chart, review the rules, and have pairs play the game several times, keeping a record of the score of each game.

Social Emphasis
Be fair and caring when relating to others.

Be aware that some students may be challenged by the mental computation in this activity, particularly when adding the sum of each roll to the ongoing total. Encourage students to use whatever methods make sense to them. Some students may need to keep track of their thinking on paper. Some strategies you might hear include:

- Decomposing numbers (for example, 35 + 8 = ?, 35 + 5 = 40, 40 + 3 = 43)
- Adding tens, then ones (for example, 16 + 25 = ?, 10 + 20 = 30, 6 + 5 = 11, 30 + 11 = 41)
- Counting by ones (for example, 43 + 8 = ? 43, 44, 45, 46...51)

Observe pairs and ask questions such as:

Q. How did you figure out that [25] and [16] is [41]? Did you both compute it the same way? If not, what was the other way you figured it out?

Q. How are you sharing the work? How are you helping each other?

●●

In pairs, students play "Fifty or More."

After pairs have played the game several times, ask pairs to report their highest total, and record the totals where all can see.

●● ●●

●● ●●

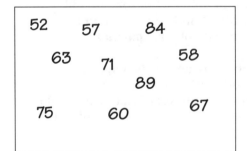

Mathematical Emphasis

The relative magnitude of numbers can be described.

Refer to the numbers and ask questions such as:

Q. Which total is the highest? Which is lowest? Are there more than or less than 20 points between the highest and lowest total? Explain.

Notes	Teacher	Students

Q. Did anyone have a total between [60 and 89]? What is the total? Is it closer to [60] or to [89]? How do you know?

•• ••

•• ••

Q. If we add all these numbers together, would the total be greater than or less than 150? 200? How do you know?

Q. What did we do with numbers in this game? Why is it important to practice adding numbers together?

Help students reflect on the lesson by asking them to think about ways they shared the work and were considerate of each other. Have pairs discuss their thinking with each other, then with the class if they wish to do so. If appropriate, share some of your observations of the ways you saw students sharing the work.

Save the "Fifty or More" rules chart for use in Lesson 8.

To provide students further opportunities to reflect on the mathematics they explored while playing "Fifty or More," have them investigate the Extensions For the Next Day before going on to the next lesson.

Extensions

For Pairs That Finish Early

■ Have pairs play "Fifty or More" again.

For the Next Day

■ Have pairs play "Fifty or More" again. As a class, read and discuss the question on the "Fifty or More: Extension" record sheet. Have each student respond to the question in writing. Provide time for partners to share their responses with each other, and then ask several pairs to share with the class. Have students place the record sheet in their Math Games Folder.

■ Continue with the ongoing "Dice Toss" Activities 1–5 described in the Overview, p. 63.

Fifty or More
Score Sheet

Roll	Total

Fifty or More

Rules

1. Roll 3 dice.

2. If you roll double or triple 1s, 2s, 4s, or 5s, add the numbers that make the double or triple and record the total on the "Fifty or More" score sheet.

3. If you roll double or triple 3s, subtract all your points and go back to 0.

4. If you roll double 6s, add 25 points. If you roll triple 6s, add 50 points.

5. Continue to roll and record until you reach a total of 50 or more points.

Materials

❏ 3 dice

❏ "Fifty or More" score sheet

❏ Paper and pencil

What are some numbers you added together as you played "Fifty or More"? Why is it important to practice adding numbers together? When do you add numbers outside of school?

Take Out Twos

Students mentally add 2-digit numbers as they play a game with three dice.

DAYS AHEAD
1

Mathematical Emphasis

In this lesson, students

- Mentally add 2-digit numbers.
- Estimate informally.
- Compare quantities.

Students add to their understanding that

- Numbers can be composed and decomposed.
- Addition and subtraction can be carried out in a variety of ways to arrive at an accurate solution.
- The relative magnitude of numbers can be described.

Social Emphasis

In this lesson, students

- Share the work.
- Share materials.
- Explain their thinking.
- Explore ways to be considerate of each other.

Students continue to

- Develop group skills.
- Relate the values of fairness, caring, and responsibility to behavior.
- Be fair and caring when relating to others.

Group Size: 2

Teacher Materials

- "Take Out Twos" rules chart (see Before the Lesson)
- 3 dice
- Transparency of "Take Out Twos" score sheet and marker

Student Materials

Each pair needs

- 3 dice and mat
- "Take Out Twos" score sheet(s)

Extension Materials

Each pair needs

- "Take Out Twos" game materials, including score sheet(s)

Each student needs

- "Take Out Twos: Extension" record sheet
- Math Games Folder

We have to take out twos, so that leaves us with 9.

24 plus 9 is the same as 24 plus 10 minus 1... so that's 24... 34... 33.

- Copy the "Take Out Twos" score sheet and cut apart so you have a score sheet for each pair, plus a few extra.

- Make a "Take Out Twos" rules chart, such as the one below, and post.

Take Out Twos

1. Roll three dice and take out any twos. (Once a die is removed, it is not rolled again in this round.)

2. Add the numbers on the remaining dice and record the results.

3. Continue rolling, adding, and recording for a total of five rolls, or until you are out of dice.

Notes

Teacher

Introduce the lesson by explaining that pairs will use three dice to play a game called "Take Out Twos." Explain that in this game students will have another opportunity to practice mentally adding the numbers they roll with the dice. Ask:

Q. What did you do with the three dice in the "Fifty or More" game? What kind of numbers were you adding?

Model "Take Out Twos" with a student as your partner.

1. Roll the dice and remove any twos. (Once a die showing a two is removed, it is set aside and not rolled again in the round.)

2. Add the numbers on the remaining dice, and record the total on the "Take Out Twos" score sheet transparency.

3. Have your partner roll the remaining dice, take out twos, and add the numbers left to the previous total.

4. Continue taking turns with your partner rolling the dice, taking out twos, and adding the remaining numbers for a total of five turns or until you are out of dice.

Students

•• ••

•• ••

Notes	Teacher	Students

Teacher

Model the game again by having the class, in pairs, keep score as you roll the dice. As the game is played, discuss the strategies students use to find the totals.

Have pairs discuss how they worked together as they played the game "Fifty or More" in the previous lesson. Ask questions such as:

Q. How did you help each other in the game "Fifty or More"? How might you help each other while playing "Take Out Twos"?

Q. How might you and your partner both be responsible for finding the totals?

Refer to the posted "Take Out Twos" rules chart, and review the rules. Have pairs play "Take Out Twos."

Students

Notes

Social Emphasis
Relate the values of fairness, caring, and responsibility to behavior.

As you observe students playing the game, ask yourself questions such as:

Q. What strategies do students use to add?
Q. How are students including each other?
Q. Have students grown in their ability to work together? How?

Mathematical Emphasis
Addition and subtraction can be carried out in a variety of ways to arrive at an accurate solution.

Teacher

Observe pairs and ask questions such as:

Q. How are you making sure you are both included in finding the totals? Does this seem to be working? If not, what might you do?

Q. (Refer to a number on their record sheet.) When you add this roll [12] to your last number [19], will you have close to [30]? Why do you think that?

Q. If you doubled this score [37], what would be your score? How did you figure it out? What is another way you could double [37]?

Q. How did you mentally add [15] and [11]? Did you both think about it the same way? Explain.

Students

In pairs, students play "Take Out Twos."

Notes	Teacher	Students

Teacher

After pairs have played several rounds of the game, ask students to look at their recorded scores. Ask questions such as:

Q. **What do you notice about your totals?**

Mathematical Emphasis
The relative magnitude of numbers can be described.

Q. **Does anyone have a score that is close to ten less than [50]? What is your score? Why do you think it is about ten less than [50]?**

Q. (Have a pair record their totals where all can see.) **If you added all your totals together, would you have more than or less than 100? How do you know? Do you agree with this pair's thinking? Why or why not?**

Q. **What did we do with numbers while playing "Take Out Twos" that might help us when we add numbers at other times?**

Social Emphasis
Be fair and caring when relating to others.

Q. **How did you and your partner treat each other considerately as you played the game?**

Save the "Take Out Twos" rules chart for use in Lessons 7 and 8.

To provide an opportunity for students to explain their thinking in writing and to reflect on their social interactions, have them explore the Extensions For the Next Day before going on to the next lesson.

Extensions

For Pairs That Finish Early

■ Have pairs play "Take Out Twos" again.

For the Next Day

■ Have pairs play "Take Out Twos" again. As a class, read and discuss the questions on the "Take Out Twos: Extension" record sheet. Have each student respond to the questions in writing. Provide time for partners to share their responses with each other, and then ask several pairs to share with the class. Have students place the record sheet in their Math Games Folder.

■ Continue with the ongoing "Dice Toss" Activities 1–5 described in the Overview, p. 63.

Take Out Twos
Score Sheet

Roll	Total

- -

Take Out Twos
Score Sheet

Roll	Total

Take Out Twos

Rules

1. Roll three dice and take out any twos. (Once a die is removed, it is not rolled again in this round.)

2. Add the numbers on the remaining dice and record the results.

3. Continue rolling, adding, and recording for a total of five rolls, or until you are out of dice.

Materials

❏ 3 dice

❏ "Take Out Twos" score sheet

❏ A pencil

1. Describe a strategy you used to mentally add a 2-digit number to another number.

2. Write about several things that helped you and your partner work well together as you played "Take Out Twos."

What's Your Game?

Students change the rules for "Take Out Twos" to create a new game in which they use mental computation to add the numbers they roll with dice. This lesson may take more than one class period.

Mathematical Emphasis

In this lesson, students

- Mentally add.
- Estimate informally.
- Compare quantities.

Students add to their understanding that

- Problems may have more than one solution and may be solved in a variety of ways.
- The relative magnitude of numbers can be described.

Social Emphasis

In this lesson, students

- Share ideas.
- Make decisions.
- Reach agreement.

Students continue to

- Develop group skills.
- Analyze the effect of behavior on others and on the group work.

Group Size: 2

Teacher Materials

- "Take Out Twos" rules chart (from Lesson 6)

Student Materials

Each pair needs

- 12" x 18" sheet of drawing paper
- Access to game materials
- Paper and a pencil

Extension Materials

Each pair needs

- Rules and materials for their game

| **Notes** | **Teacher** | **Students** |

Post the "Take Out Twos" rules chart from the prior lesson.

Refer to the "Take Out Twos" rules chart and review the game students played in the previous lesson. Ask:

Q. What was challenging about playing "Take Out Twos"?

Q. What mathematics did you use to play "Take Out Twos"?

Q. How do you think the game might be different if you used [two] dice instead of three? Explain.

Q. How else could you change the rules of "Take Out Twos"? How might your results change if you changed a rule in that way?

Students might suggest taking out a different number, rolling the dice fewer than or more than five times, or using a different number of dice (for example, use two dice rather than three).

Explain that partners will change the "Take Out Twos" game and have further practice computing mentally as they play each other's games. As a class, change the "Take Out Twos" game using four dice. Record the name of the new game, the rules, and the materials needed where all can see. For example:

Take Out Ones

1. Roll 4 dice and take out ones.

2. Add the remaining numbers and record.

3. Continue rolling, adding, and recording for a total of ten rolls, or until you run out of dice.

Ask pairs to create their own new game, based on "Take Out Twos," and to record the name of the game, the rules, and the materials needed on a sheet of drawing paper. Have pairs play their new game several times and keep a record of their rolls and totals for each game.

Notes	Teacher	Students

As you observe students working, ask yourself questions such as:

Q. What predictions do students make about how their game's totals might be different than "Take Out Twos"? What reasons do they give for their predictions?

Q. What strategies do students use to compute the totals? Are they using a wider variety of strategies now than they were at the beginning of the unit?

Observe pairs working and ask questions such as:

Q. **What are the rules for your game? How are they different from "Take Out Twos"?**

Q. **How do you think the totals for your ["Take Out Fives"] game might be different from "Take Out Twos"?**

Q. **How did you find the total for [27] and [14]?**

•• In pairs, students

1. Make up a new game based on "Take Out Twos."

2. Record the name of the game, the rules, and the materials needed on a sheet of drawing paper.

3. Play the new game several times, recording the rolls and totals for each game.

You may want to do this part of the lesson during another class period. If so, make sure pairs save their game and totals.

After pairs have played their new game a few times, ask several pairs to share their game with the class. Discuss questions such as:

Q. **How did you change the game? How many other pairs changed the game by changing the [number of rolls of the dice]? What happened?**

Q. **What other changes did pairs make?**

Ask several pairs to share one of their totals, and record these where all can see. For example:

•• ••

•• ••

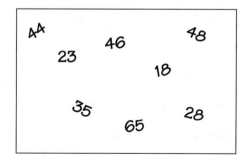

Notes	Teacher	Students

Teacher

Ask questions such as:

Q. Which of these numbers added together have a sum close to [100]? How do you know? More than [200]? How do you know?

Q. What two numbers have a difference of about [20]? How did you figure it out?

Help students reflect on ways they came to decisions about the rules for their new game by discussing questions such as:

Q. How did you and your partner come to agreement about the rules for your game? How did other pairs come to agreement? Why did this seem to work?

Q. What problems did you have making decisions? How did the problems affect your work? How did this affect how you felt?

Q. How were you able to solve the problems and reach agreement? What might you do differently next time?

Collect pairs' "What's Your Game?" rules charts for use in the Extensions For the Next Day. Have them explore the Extensions For the Next Day before going on to the next lesson.

Students

•• ••

•• ••

Notes

Mathematical Emphasis
The relative magnitude of numbers can be described.

Social Emphasis
Analyze the effect of behavior on others and on the group work.

Extensions

For Pairs That Finish Early

■ Have pairs play their new game again.

For the Next Day

■ Have pairs exchange their "What's Your Game?" rules charts. Have pairs read the other pair's game rules, get the necessary materials, and play the game several times. Ask pairs to think about the two games and to discuss ways their games are similar and ways they are different.

■ Continue with the ongoing "Dice Toss" Activities 1–5 described in the Overview, p. 63.

Favorite Games

DAYS AHEAD
1
TRANSITION

Students create a class graph about their favorite games in the unit and analyze and discuss the collected data. Students reflect on and write about their experiences in the unit.

Teacher Materials

- Blank chart paper
- Charts of game rules from previous lessons

Student Materials

Each pair needs

- Self-stick note
- A pencil

Each student needs

- "Favorite Games" record sheet
- Math Games Folder

Extension Materials

Each student needs

- Math Games Folder
- Materials for playing games (see Before the Lesson)

Transition Emphasis

In this lesson, students

- Review the games they played.
- Graph and interpret data.
- Make statements about the data.
- Reflect on how they worked together.

Students add to their understanding that

- Questions about our world can be asked, and data about those questions can be collected, organized, and analyzed.
- Problems may have more than one solution and may be solved in a variety of ways.
- Numbers can be used to describe quantities.

Social Emphasis

In this lesson, students

- Make decisions.
- Reach agreement.

Students continue to

- Develop group skills.
- Be fair and caring when relating to others.
- Analyze the effect of behavior on others and on the group work.

Group Size: 2

■ If you choose to do the Extension For the Future, you may want to make plastic bags of materials for each of the games from the unit and allow students to check them out to use at home.

Notes	Teacher	Students

Notes

Post the sheet of blank chart paper. Display all game rules charts from the unit:

■ "Exactly 100"
■ "Cover the Coins"
■ "Close to 100"
■ "Fifty or More"
■ "Take Out Twos"
■ Pairs' created games

Social Emphasis

Be fair and caring when relating to others.

Teacher

Introduce the lesson by referring to the posted game rules charts and asking questions such as:

Q. What do you remember about ["Exactly 100"]? What else can we say about this game?

Q. What kind of mathematics did we do in ["Close to 100"]?

Q. Which games were the most fun for you to play with your partner? Why?

Q. Which games were the most difficult? Why?

Explain that partners will discuss the games they played in the unit, choose one game they both liked, and record the name of the game in large letters on a self-stick note. Discuss questions such as:

Q. What might you do so that you can come to agreement about a game you both liked? Why do you think this might be a fair way to choose?

Q. What other ideas do you have?

Students

•• ••

•• ••

Observe how students discuss their ideas and come to agreement. Note positive interactions and any problems you might discuss when the class reflects on the lesson.

Observe students and ask questions such as:

Q. Which game did you choose? Why do you both like this game?

Q. How did you come to agreement on ["Close to 100"]? Why do you think this was a fair way to come to agreement?

•• In pairs, students

1. Discuss the games in the unit.

2. Agree on a game they both like.

3. Write the name of this game in large letters on a self-stick note.

After all pairs have recorded a game on a self-stick note, have pairs post their note on the chart paper. Have several pairs explain why they chose the game.

•• ••

•• ••

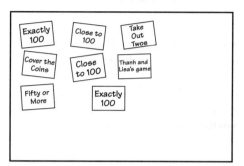

A cooperative strategy such as "Think, Pair, Share" (see p. xii) can provide opportunities for all students to reflect on a problem before discussing their thinking.

Refer to the collected data and facilitate a discussion about how the class might organize the data by asking questions such as:

Q. How might we organize our data? What other ideas do you have?

Use one student's suggestion for organizing the data and arrange it accordingly. For example:

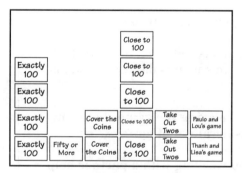

Notes	Teacher	Students

Mathematical Emphasis

Questions about our world can be asked, and data about these questions can be collected, organized, and analyzed.

Have the class decide on a title and label the graph. Analyze the collected data by having students, first in pairs, then as a class, make statements about the data. Record students' statements where all can see.

After several statements have been recorded, ask questions such as:

Q. Did less than half or more than half of the class choose "Close to 100" as their favorite game? How do you know?

Q. If twice as many students chose "Fifty or More," how many students would that be? How do you know?

Q. How many students are represented on this graph? Explain. How can we make this clear to people reading our graph?

Help students reflect on the mathematics they explored during the unit by asking:

Q. Why do you think we have been playing these games? What have they helped you learn how to do?

Social Emphasis

Analyze the effect of behavior on others and on the group work.

To help students reflect on their work in the unit, have students discuss questions such as:

Q. How did playing the games help you be considerate of others?

Q. How did working with a partner help you learn?

As a class, read the questions on the "Favorite Games" record sheet. Have each student respond to the questions in writing. Provide time for partners to share their responses with each other, and then ask several pairs to share with the class. Have students place their record sheet in their Math Games Folder.

You may want to share your observations about how partners and the class worked together in this lesson and during the unit.

Extensions

For Pairs That Finish Early

■ Have students share their Math Games Folder with their partner.

For the Future

■ Have students take their Math Games Folder home and share it with a family member or family friend. Encourage students to play the games at home by sending game materials home with students. After students have had a chance to play the games at home, provide class time for them to share their experiences.

Favorite Games

A game we both liked was _____ .
My partner and I chose this game because

_____

_____

_____ .

1. What have you learned about numbers and mathematics by playing these games?

2. What have you learned about working with a partner by playing these games?

Informal Computation

Mathematical Development

This unit provides students with experiences that help them develop and practice addition and subtraction strategies. Students have opportunities to find sums and differences using mental computation as well as counters, the Hundred Chart, or paper-and-pencil methods. They have informal experiences solving computation problems with Number Cards and data, as well as more structured opportunities to individually solve addition and subtraction problems, verbalize their strategies, and listen to and record their own strategies or the strategies they hear. These experiences provide students with practice in clearly communicating their mathematical thinking verbally and in writing, which in turn supports the ongoing development of their reasoning and flexibility with computation.

Mathematical Emphasis

Conceptually, experiences in this unit help students construct their understanding that

- Operations can be carried out in a variety of ways to arrive at an accurate solution.

- Making a reasonable estimate requires gathering and using information.

- The relative magnitude of numbers can be described.

- Numbers can be composed and decomposed.

- Problems may have more then one solution and may be solved in a variety of ways.

- Questions about our world can be asked, and data about those questions can be collected, organized, and analyzed.

- Numbers can be used to describe quantities.

Social Development

In this unit, students continue to develop their cooperative skills, particularly ways to respect the time others need to think; to listen to and include each other's ideas and strategies; and to be responsible participants in group activities. Open-ended questions encourage students to examine how the underlying values of fairness, caring, and responsibility relate to behavior and why they are important.

Students are randomly assigned to groups of four that work together in Lessons 1, 2, and 7. In Lessons 3, 4, 5, and 6, groups are divided into pairs.

Social Emphasis

Socially, experiences in this unit help students to

- Develop group skills.

- Analyze why it is important to be fair, caring, and responsible.

- Relate the values of fairness, caring, and responsibility to behavior.

- Analyze the effect of behavior on others and on the group work.

- Take responsibility for learning and behavior.

- Be fair and caring when relating to others.

This unit includes seven lessons and an ongoing informal computation activity. The calendar icon indicates that some preparation is needed or that an experience is suggested for the students prior to that lesson.

1. Letters, Letters, Letters
(page 129)

Team-building lesson in which groups discuss and compare their first names and make a graph of the letters in their first names.

2. How Many Letters?
(page 137)

Problem-solving lesson in which students determine the total number of letters in all the first names in the class.

3. First and Last Names 1
(page 143)

Informal computation lesson in which students use the number of letters in their first and last names to estimate and solve addition problems.

4. First and Last Names 2
(page 149)

Informal computation lesson in which pairs solve addition problems and record each other's strategies.

5. Tea Party!
(page 153)

Informal computation lesson in which students estimate and find the difference between pairs of numbers.

6. What's the Difference?
(page 157)

Informal computation lesson in which students compare pairs of numbers, subtract, and write about the differences.

7. Stupendous Students
(page 161)

Transition lesson in which students reflect on and write about their mathematical and social experiences during the unit.

Number Card Activity

This ongoing activity provides opportunities for students to informally compute, estimate, and share strategies with their partner and with the class. Begin this activity after Lesson 3.

Prior to Lesson 3, make yourself a set of cards with 1- and 2-digit numbers using fifteen to twenty 4″ × 6″ index cards. For example:

Use the cards for short informal computation and estimation activities. Show two or more cards at a time and ask students questions such as:

Q. **If we add these two numbers, is the total more than or less than [20]? How do you know?**

Q. **What is the total of these two numbers? How do you know? What is the difference between these two numbers? Explain.**

Q. **If we add these three numbers together, do you think the total will be more than or less than [50]? Explain.**

Q. **If we add these four numbers together, do you think the total will be more than or less than [100]? Explain.**

For each question, have students individually solve the problem, then share their strategy with a partner. Have several pairs share their strategies with the class.

Materials

The materials needed for the unit are listed below. The first page of each lesson lists the materials specific to that lesson. Blackline masters for group record sheets are included at the end of each lesson.

Throughout the unit, you will need an overhead projector, overhead pens, and markers. Students will need access to supplies, such as counters, interlocking cubes, scissors, crayons, glue sticks, paper, and pencils. If possible, each group should have a container with these supplies available to use at their discretion. Students willl not need calculators in this unit.

Teacher Materials

- Materials for forming groups (Lesson 1)
- 5 grid strips (Lesson 1)
- 12″ × 18″ sheet of construction paper (Lesson 1)
- Glue stick (Lesson 1)
- Scissors (Lesson 1)
- Chart Paper (Lessons 2, 6)
- Adhesive dots (Lesson 2)
- "Number of Letters in Our First Names" reference sheet (Lesson 2)
- 4″ × 6″ index cards (Lesson 3)
- Pocket chart (Lessons 3, 4)
- Paper lunch bag with Number Cards for each pair (Lesson 6)
- 12″ × 18″ sheets of drawing paper (Lesson 7)

Student Materials

Each group of four needs:

- 12″ × 18″ sheet of construction paper (Lesson 1)
- Glue stick (Lesson 1)
- Scissors (Lesson 1)
- Paper folder (Lesson 1)
- Access to a dictionary (Lesson 7)
- Group folder (Lessons 2, 7)

Each pair needs

- Group folder (Lessons 3, 4, 5, 6)
- 4″ × 6″ index cards (Lesson 3)
- Counters and Hundred Chart (Lessons 3, 4, 6)
- Paper clip (Lesson 3)

Each student needs

- A grid strip (Lesson 1)
- Counters and Hundred Chart (Lesson 2)
- Self-portrait page (Lesson 7)

Extension Materials

- Pocket chart (Lesson 3)
- Class book, "Stupendous Students" (Lesson 7)

Each group of four needs

- "Number of Letters in Our First Names" reference sheet (Lesson 2)
- "Ms. Trott's Second Grade" reference sheet (Lesson 2)
- Counters and Hundred Chart (Lesson 2)

Each pair needs

- Group folder (Lesson 4)
- Paper lunch bag with Number Cards (Lesson 6)
- Counters and Hundred Chart (Lesson 6)

Each student needs

- Group folder (Lesson 5)

Teaching Hints

- The primary focus of this unit is to help students develop their own strategies for adding and subtracting numbers. To help students construct their own approaches and understanding, allow time for each student to think privately prior to sharing their methods with a partner or the class.

- Students are frequently asked to verbalize their thinking in this unit. Keep in mind that while some strategies may seem to be more appropriate or efficient than others, it is important to allow students to carry out procedures that make sense to them, and to avoid emphasizing one strategy or way of thinking over another. Avoid intervening too quickly when students seem to be using an inefficient strategy or are heading toward what seems to be an incorrect answer. Instead, probe their thinking using open-ended questions.

- To help students connect oral and written explanations, take opportunities to record students' computation strategies where all can see. For example:

> First I added the 20 and the 40 and got 60. Then I added 7 plus 6. That's 13. I added 60 and 13 and got 73.

$$27 + 46$$
$$20 + 40 = 60$$
$$7 + 6 = 13$$
$$60 + 13 = 73$$

- Some students may need to use counters, interlocking cubes, or a Hundred Chart to help them informally compute. Make these available for students to use as needed.

- In this unit, students keep their work in group folders introduced at the end of Lesson 1. At the end of the unit, students will use the work in their folders for discussion and written reflection.

Assessment Techniques

In this unit, students construct their understandings of strategies for informal computation. The following informal assessment techniques will help you assess your students' understandings of number composition and decomposition, number relationships, and how operations can be carried out in a variety of ways. Students' understandings and approaches in computation are likely to vary from experience to experience, particularly as students are developing number and operations concepts.

Before each lesson, select some of the suggested open-ended questions to ask your students to explore their mathematical and social understanding, or develop questions of your own. Be ready to probe students' thinking during the lesson by asking follow-up questions that require them to explain further (for example, *How do you know? Say more about that. What do you mean by ___?*) Keep in mind that students' ability to clearly verbalize their thinking does not always match their conceptual understanding. Encourage students to communicate their thinking the best they can, perhaps helping them think about how they would explain their idea to a younger student, or encouraging them to use pictures, diagrams, or manipulatives. Remember that, like most communication skills, students' ability to verbalize their thinking improves with opportunities to practice over time.

Note that many lessons have an assessment section in the notes column with specific questions you can ask yourself as you observe your students. Whenever possible, record students' responses and compare them over time to assess growth in conceptual understanding. As you observe students throughout the unit, consider using the assessment questions below. Note change in students' conceptual understanding as well as their behavior; for example, *Does the student exhibit confidence in his or her own mathematical thinking? Is he or she able to persevere? Does the student give up easily, suggesting a belief that he or she lacks the ability to solve the problem? If so, does the student experience success and demonstrate more confidence as the unit progresses?*

Observe Individual Students Working

As you observe and listen to students, ask yourself questions such as:

Q. What strategies does the student use to solve addition problems?

For solving a problem like 35 + 17 = ___, students may use stratgies such as:

- **decomposing numbers** (students may decompose the 17 into 10 and 7 and think "35 + 10 = 45, 45 + 7 = 52");

- **making one number "friendlier" to the other** ("turn 17 into 20, and add 35 + 20 = 55, 55 - 3 = 52");

- **adding tens and ones separately** ("30 + 10 = 40, 5 + 7 = 12, 40 + 10 = 50, 50 + 2 = 52");

- **using a Hundred Chart** ("starting at 35, go down one row and to the right 7 spaces, or go down two rows and to the left 3 spaces");

- simply **counting** by ones, twos, fives, tens, etc. ("35, 40, 45, 50, 51, 52, 53").

One way students demonstrate that the strategies they are using make sense to them is by talking about numbers as quantities ("I added 5 and 7 and got 12, then I took the 10 from 12 and added it to the 40") rather than symbols being manipulated ("I added 5 and 7, wrote down a 2, and carried a 1").

Q. What strategies does the student use to find the difference between two numbers?

To solve 41 - 23 = ___, students might:

- **add up** from the subtrahend ("23 + 10 = 33, 33 + 7 = 40, 40 + 1 = 41, so 10 + 7 + 1 = 18" or "23 + 20 = 43, 43 - 2 = 41, so 20 - 2 = 18");

- **take away** ("41 - 20 = 21, 21 - 3 = 18");

- **deal with tens and ones separately** ("40 - 20 = 20, 20 + 1 - 3 = 18");

- use **counting** by ones, twos, fives, tens, etc.

Subtraction can be used to determine what is left after taking away a quantity from a whole, and it can also be used to find the difference between two quantities. In this unit, students compare numbers and explore ways to find the difference between them.

Q. How does the student demonstrate fairness, caring, and responsibility when working with others?

Observe students as they work and note how a student takes responsibility for his or her behavior and interaction with others. *How is the student respectful of others' thinking and ideas? How does the student include others and handle disagreements in fair and caring ways? How does the student participate and share ideas during the reflection at the end of each lesson?*

Reflect on Your Role as Teacher

As you reflect on your role in each lesson, consider the following questions:

Q. Did I allow time for students to reason through and explain their own strategies, or did I inadvertently impose my thinking? Did I ask open-ended questions? Did I encourage a variety of responses? How did I handle the unexpected?

Q. Did I allow enough time for each student to think and develop their own understandings before I asked students to answer questions and discuss their thinking? Did I encourage students to give each other time to think before sharing ideas? How did I encourage students to listen to each other's thinking?

Q. Did I ask open-ended questions? How did I encourage a variety of responses? Was I unbiased about students' responses? How did I handle the unexpected?

Q. What part of the lesson would I change the next time? Why?

Student Writing

Throughout the unit, students are asked to verbalize their thinking and at times, to explain their thinking in writing. During this unit, students write

- Statements about data on graphs.
- Explanations of their strategies for solving problems.
- Their partner's strategies for solving problems.
- Reflections about their work in the unit.

Letters, Letters, Letters

Students use the letters in their first names to make a group graph, then view, discuss, and write statements about the data. This lesson may take more than one class period.

Mathematical Emphasis

In this lesson, students

- Collect, organize, and analyze data.
- Write statements about data.

Students add to their understanding that

- Questions about our world can be asked, and data about those questions can be collected, organized, and analyzed.

Social Emphasis

In this lesson, students

- Include everyone.
- Share the work.
- Move responsibly around the room.

Students continue to

- Develop group skills.
- Take responsibility for learning and behavior.
- Relate the values of fairness, caring, and responsibility to behavior.

Group Size: 4

Teacher Materials

- Materials for forming groups (see Before the Lesson)
- 5 grid strips (see Before the Lesson)
- 12″ × 18″ sheet of construction paper (see Before the Lesson)
- Scissors
- Glue stick

Student Materials

Each student needs

- A grid strip (see Before the Lesson)
- Marker

Each group of four needs

- 12″ × 18″ sheet of construction paper
- Scissors
- Glue stick
- Paper and a pencil
- Paper folder

Extension Materials

Each group needs

- "First Name Letters" graph (from the lesson)

■ Make copies of the "Grid Paper" blackline master and cut into strips. You will need five strips for yourself and one strip for each student.

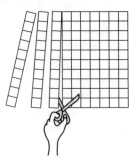

■ Using a marker, make four sample name strips by writing your first name and the first names of three friends in capital letters on the strips, with one letter in each square. For example:

Cut apart the letters in each name strip and glue them in alphabetical order onto a 12″ × 18″ sheet of construction paper labeled "First Name Letters." For example:

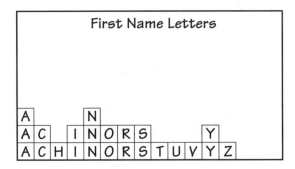

■ Make a second sample name strip for yourself and do not cut it apart.

SHARON

■ If your students are not familiar with the "Stroll and Stop" strategy (see p. xii), have them practice it in groups of four prior to the lesson. Discuss how groups might move around the room in a responsible way.

■ Decide how you will forms groups (see Forming Groups, p. xiii, for random grouping suggestions). Prepare any materials needed.

Randomly assign students to groups of four. Explain that at times in this unit students will be working in this group and at times in pairs.

Social Emphasis
Develop group skills.

Students might say:

- "Our first names have the same number of letters."
- "My name is the only one in the group with a 'Y' in it."
- "We all have two-syllable names."

Introduce the lesson by explaining that in this unit students will help each other learn more about how to solve addition and subtraction problems and to collect, organize, and analyze data about their names. Explain that they will work in groups of four as well as with a partner in the group. As a class, discuss questions such as:

Q. **How might it be different to work in a group of four compared to with a partner?**

Q. **What have you learned about working together with a partner that might help you work with a group of four?**

Explain that in this lesson groups will make a graph of the letters in their first names. Show your name strip and share some information about your name, such as how you were named, what your name means, or a nickname you have. Then, ask questions such as:

Q. **What do you know about your name? Does your name have special meaning? If so, what?**

Q. **Does anyone you know have the same first name as you? Who?**

Explain that students will write their first name in capital letters on a grid strip, one letter in each square. Ask students to then discuss the similarities and differences in their first names. Distribute a grid strip to each student.

Observe groups and ask questions such as:

Q. How are your names the same? How are they different?

Q. How do you know the members in your group are listening to each other? Is there something you'd like to change about how you are working together?

●● In groups, students

1. Individually write their first name in capital letters on a grid strip, one letter in each square.

2. Discuss the similarities and differences in their names.

Have several groups share what they found out about their names. Ask questions such as:

Q. What was the same about your names? What was different?

Q. Did you find something that is special about your names? Explain.

Display your "First Name Letters" graph.

First Name Letters

A			N									
A	C		I	N	O	R	S				Y	
A	C	H	I	N	O	R	S	T	U	V	Y	Z

Referring to the graph, explain that you used the letters in your first name and in three friends' names to make this graph. Ask:

Q. What do you notice about this graph?

Q. What do you notice about how the letters are arranged on this graph?

Notes	Teacher	Students

Teacher

Explain that each group will make their own "First Name Letters" graph by cutting apart the letters in their name strips, arranging the letters in alphabetical order, and then gluing the letters onto a sheet of construction paper. Use your sample name strip to model cutting apart the letters and arranging them in alphabetical order.

Ask groups to make their own "First Name Letters" graph.

Notes

As you observe students, ask yourself questions such as:

Q. How are students working together? Are all members actively involved?
Q. How are they sharing materials?

Teacher

Observe groups working and ask questions such as:

Q. Which letter do you think will occur most often on your graph? Why? Which letter do you think might occur most often on all the graphs? Why?

Q. What can you say so far about your group's graph?

Q. What are you doing to make sure you are sharing the work?

Students

•• In groups, students

1. Cut apart their strips.

2. Arrange the letters in alphabetical order on a sheet of construction paper and glue the letters in place.

Notes

You may want to do this part of the lesson during another class period.

For example, some statements might be:

■ "A" and "N" are the most common letters on the graph.
■ "E" is the only vowel not on the graph.

Teacher

After groups have finished making their graphs, refer to your "First Name Letters" graph and ask:

Q. What statements might we make about this graph? Explain.

As students make statements, write them where all can see.

Explain that groups will stroll around the room and, on a signal, stop to discuss a graph and write a group statement about the data. Review the "Stroll and Stop" strategy and discuss how students might stroll about the room in a responsible way. Discuss questions such as:

Q. What might your group do before moving to a graph?

Students

•• ••
•• ••
•• ••

Social Emphasis
Take responsibility for learning and behavior.

Q. If you need to wait for a group to finish, how might you do so in a considerate way? What might you do while you are waiting?

Q. How can you make sure everyone is included in the discussion and the work?

Q. What do you need to do before you write your group statement? How can you help each other come to a decision about what to write?

Have groups stroll to several graphs. It is not necessary to have them stroll to all the graphs.

Ask groups to place their graph, a sheet of paper, and a pencil on a desk and begin the stroll.

Observe how students move around the room and discuss the graphs. Note statements on the graphs that you might like to discuss when the class reflects on the lesson.

Observe groups strolling and ask questions such as:

Q. What do you find interesting about this group's graph? How is it like your group's graph? How is it different?

Q. How are you deciding on a statement to write about this graph?

Q. How are you moving around the room in a responsible way?

In groups, students

1. Stroll around the room, stop, and look at and discuss another group's graph.

2. Write a statement about the graph.

3. On a signal, stroll to a new graph and repeat the activity.

Have students return to their seats. Ask questions such as:

Q. What did you notice about the different graphs? What letters seemed to occur most often?

Mathematical Emphasis

Questions about our world can be asked, and data about those questions can be collected, organized, and analyzed.

Display and refer to several graphs and accompanying statements and discuss questions such as:

Q. This statement says, [There are twice as many S's as M's]. Do you agree? Why? Why not?

Q. About how many letters are on this graph? Explain. Why do you think so?

Q. (Refer to two graphs.) Do you think there are more than or fewer than 50 letters on these two graphs? Why?

Help students reflect on their work together by asking questions such as:

Q. Why was it important to move around the room in a responsible way during the stroll?

Q. How did you include everyone? Did you think that was fair? Why?

Q. What problems did your group have? How did you try to solve them?

If appropriate, share some of your observations of the positive interactions and problems you noted as groups worked.

Provide each group with a paper folder to keep their work during the unit. Ask each group to place their "First Name Letters" graph in the folder.

Social Emphasis

Relate the values of fairness, caring, and responsibility to behavior.

Extensions

For Groups That Finish Early

■ Have groups discuss the data on their graphs.

For the Next Day

■ Continue with the next lesson, "How Many Letters?"

Grid Paper

How Many Letters?

Students use a graph to determine the total number of letters in all the first names in the class.

DAYS AHEAD
2

Mathematical Emphasis

In this lesson, students

- Solve a computation problem.
- Make estimates.
- Record strategies.

Students add to their understanding that

- Problems may have more than one solution and may be solved in a variety of ways.
- Operations can be carried out in a variety of ways to arrive at an accurate solution.
- Making a reasonable estimate requires gathering and using information.

Social Emphasis

In this lesson, students

- Give each other time to solve problems individually.
- Help each other when asked.
- Ask questions about the thinking of others.

Students continue to

- Develop group skills.
- Analyze why it is important to be fair, caring, and responsible.
- Analyze the effect of behavior on others and on the group work.

Group Size: 4

Teacher Materials

- Chart paper and adhesive dots (see Before the Lesson)
- "Number of Letters in Our First Names" reference sheet (see Before the Lesson)

Student Materials

Each student needs

- Paper and a pencil
- Access to counters and Hundred Chart (see Unit 1, Lesson 3)

Each group of four needs

- Group folder

Extension Materials

Each group needs

- "Number of Letters in Our First Names" reference sheet
- "Ms. Trott's Second Grade" reference sheet
- Paper and a pencil
- Access to counters and Hundred Chart

■ Make the following graph on a large sheet of chart paper and post:

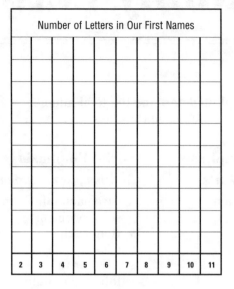

Number of Letters in Our First Names

| | | | | | | | | | |
|2|3|4|5|6|7|8|9|10|11|

■ The day before the lesson, ask each student to count the number of letters in his or her first name and place an adhesive dot on the graph in the appropriate column.

■ After the class data are collected, copy the information onto the "Number of Letters in Our First Names" reference sheet and make a copy for each student.

Notes	Teacher	Students

Notes

A cooperative structure such as "Heads Together" (see p. xii) can provide opportunities for all students to be involved in the discussion.

Teacher

Introduce the lesson by asking students what they found out about each other's names in the previous lesson. Show the "Number of Letters in Our First Names" graph and ask questions such as:

Q. **What does this graph tell us?**

Q. **What do you notice about this graph? Is there anything about the data that surprises you? What?**

Q. (Point to the 2 in the lower left hand corner.) **Why do you think this graph begins with "2"?**

Q. (Refer to the data.) **How many letters does this column show? How did you figure it out?**

Q. **Do you think there are more than or fewer than 50 letters represented on this graph? Why?**

Q. Do you think there are close to 100 letters represented on this graph? Explain.

:: ::
:: ::

Explain that groups will discuss the information on the "Number of Letters in Our First Names" graph, individually find the total number of letters in all the first names in the class, and record their own solution and strategy. Students will then share their written solutions with their group. Discuss questions such as:

Q. How might you start this problem?

Q. What are some ways you might find the total?

Q. How might the members in your group help each other? How will you know when someone needs help?

Q. How can you allow each group member time to solve the problem in his or her own way? Why is that important?

Q. What can you do to show that you are listening to the thinking of others? If you don't understand someone's thinking, how can you get more information without hurting his or her feelings? Why is that important?

Distribute the "Number of Letters in Our First Names" reference sheets and ask groups to discuss the information and ways to solve the problem. Ask students to individually solve the problem, record their strategies, and share their written solutions and strategies with their group.

Social Emphasis

Analyze why it is important to be fair, caring, and responsible.

As you observe groups working, ask yourself questions such as:

Q. What strategies are students using? Are they flexible in their thinking? If so, how?

Q. Do students persist? Do they encourage others to persist?

Q. How are groups sharing ideas?

Observe groups and ask questions such as:

Q. What strategy are you using? Does it seem to be working? How? If not, what else might you try?

Q. How are you helping each other?

Q. How are you making sure you understand each other's solutions and strategies?

:: In groups, students

1. Discuss the data and possible ways to find the total number of letters in all the first names in the class.

2. Individually find the total number of letters and record their own strategy and solution.

3. Share their strategies and solutions with each other.

Notes	Teacher	Students

Mathematical Emphasis

Problems may have more than one solution and may be solved in a variety of ways.

Social Emphasis

Analyze the effect of behavior on others and on the group work.

Have several groups explain the different strategies their individual members used. Encourage students to ask questions about the explanations. Discuss questions such as:

Q. **What did you find out? How many letters are there in all the first names in the class? How did you figure it out? What other strategies did your group members use?**

Q. **If we make a graph of our first and last names, about how many letters do you think we might have? Why do you think so?**

Help students reflect on the lesson by asking questions such as:

Q. **What went well for your group today? How did that help you in your work?**

Q. **What didn't work so well today? What can you and your group do next time to make things work better?**

Q. **What happened when the members of your group finished their work at different times? How did that affect the others in the group?**

Q. **How did it feel to have others in your group ask questions about your thinking?**

Ask students to place their work in their group folder. Save the "Number of Letters in Our First Names" graph for use in Lesson 7.

Extensions

For Students Who Finish Early

- Have students find and record another way they could solve the problem.

For the Next Day

- Have groups take their "Number of Letters in Our First Names" reference sheet out of their group folder. Explain that they will compare the data from their class with that of another second grade class. Distribute the "Mrs. Trott's Second Grade" reference sheets and ask groups to discuss and compare the data on the two graphs. As groups share their observations with the class, discuss their statements and record them where all can see.

Number of Letters in Our First Names

2	3	4	5	6	7	8	9	10	11

Ms. Trott's Second Grade

Number of Letters in Our First Names

2	3	4	5	6	7	8	9	10	11
			●						
			●						
			●						
		●	●	●	●				
		●	●	●	●				
		●	●	●	●		●		
	●	●	●	●	●	●	●		
●	●	●	●	●	●	●	●		●

First and Last Names 1

Students practice mentally and informally adding numbers using Number Cards. This lesson may take more than one class period.

DAYS AHEAD
1

Mathematical Emphasis

In this lesson, students

- Solve addition problems mentally and informally.
- Use a variety of computational strategies.
- Make estimates.

Students add to their understanding that

- Operations can be carried out in a variety of ways to arrive at an accurate solution.
- Making a reasonable estimate requires gathering and using information.
- The relative magnitude of numbers can be described.

Social Emphasis

In this lesson, students

- Give each other time to solve problems individually.
- Explain their thinking.
- Listen to each other.

Students continue to

- Develop group skills.
- Relate the values of fairness, caring, and responsibility to behavior.

Group Size: 2

Teacher Materials

- 4″ × 6″ index cards (see Before the Lesson)
- Pocket chart

Student Materials

Each pair needs

- 4″ × 6″ index cards and a pencil
- Access to group folder
- Access to counters and Hundred Chart (see Unit 1, Lesson 3)
- Paper clip

Extension Materials

- Pocket chart
- Pairs' Number Cards (from the lesson)

■ Have each student make two Number Cards by recording the number of letters in their first name one one index card and the number of letters in their first and last names combined on a second index card. Have students write their names on the back of the cards. Make two cards for yourself. For example:

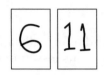

[Sharon] [Sharon Trott]

When students have finished making their cards, facilitate a discussion about the number of letters on their Number Cards by asking questions such as:

Q. **Who has more than** [ten] **letters in their first and last names combined?** (Have these students raise their hands or stand.) **Is this more than or less than half of our class? Explain.**

Q. (Hold up a student's cards.) **How many more letters are in** [Tamar's] **first and last names than in her first name? How do you know?**

Q. **If you doubled the number of letters in your first name, how many letters would you have? How do you know? In your first and last names?**

Following the class discussion, have students put their Number Cards into their group folder.

Notes	Teacher	Students
Divide groups into pairs.	**R**eview the addition problem students solved in the previous lesson. Explain that students will help each other add the numbers on their Number Cards to make new cards. Model the activity by placing your Number Cards in a pocket chart. Ask students to find the sum of the numbers on the cards, then share their solution with their partner. As a class, discuss the different ways students found the sum.	●● ●● ●● ●●

Write the sum on an index card, and add this Number Card to the pocket chart. For example:

•• ••

•• ••

Repeat the activity using a student's set of Number Cards. For example:

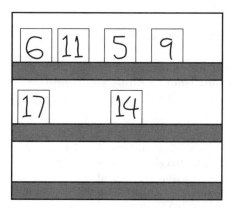

Continue to make new Number Cards by combining any of the cards on the chart in a variety of ways. For example:

Notice that in this example, 16 can be made by combining 11 and 5, 25 can be made by combining 16 and 9, 36 can be made by adding 20 and 16, and 45 can be made by adding 16, 14, 9, and 6.

A cooperative structure such as "Think, Pair, Share" (see p. xii) can provide opportunities for all students to reflect on a problem before discussing their thinking.

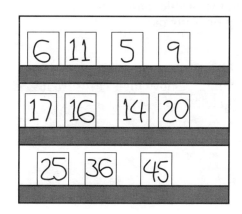

Discuss questions such as:

•• ••

•• ••

Mathematical Emphasis

Operations can be carried out in a variety of ways to arrive at an accurate solution.

Q. What is another way to combine some of these numbers? How did you figure it out? Did someone do it a different way? Explain.

Q. What is a way to put three of these numbers together? What is the total? How did you figure it out? Did someone do it a different way? Explain.

Some students may need to use counters or a Hundred Chart to help them solve the problems.

Explain that pairs will combine the numbers on their Number Cards in a variety of ways to find new sums. Each new sum will be recorded on an index card and added to their set of Number Cards.

Facilitate a class discussion about how partners can give each other time to individually add the numbers before sharing solutions. Discuss questions such as:

Social Emphasis

Relate the values of fairness, caring, and responsibility to behavior.

Q. Why is it important that you give each other time to think about and solve the problem?

Q. If you are adding numbers together, how can you be considerate of your partner who might need more time than you to solve the problem?

Q. What can you do if your partner is ready and you need more time?

Q. What might you do if you are finished solving the problem and you are waiting for your partner to finish? How is this being a responsible learner?

Ask partners to remove their cards from their group folder and begin the activity.

As you observe students working, ask yourself questions such as:

Q. What strategies are students using to find the totals?

Q. How are students being responsible for their own learning?

Observe pairs and ask questions such as:

Q. **If you add these two numbers together, what is the sum? How do you know?**

Q. **Can you make [30] with your numbers? Explain.**

Q. **How are you making sure you are both solving the problem?**

Q. **What strategies did each of you use to find the sums?**

•• In pairs, students

1. Combine two or more numbers in their set of Number Cards and individually find the sum.

2. Share their solutions and thinking, agree on the sum, then record it on an index card.

3. Add the new card to their set of Number Cards and repeat the activity.

You may want to do this part of the lesson during another class period.

Display one pair's set of Number Cards. For example:

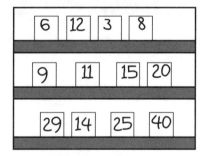

•• ••

•• ••

Ask question such as:

Q. **What do you notice about this pair's Number Cards?**

Q. **How do you think the students in this pair made [14]? How do you think they made [25]? Explain.**

Q. **Can some of these numbers be put together to make a number close to [50]? Explain.**

Mathematical Emphasis

The relative magnitude of numbers can be described.

Q. **If we added all these numbers together, do you think the total would be more than or less than 100? Explain.**

Q. **What are some ways you have found to easily add the numbers together?**

Notes	**Teacher**	**Students**

Help students reflect on their work
together by asking questions such as:

**Q. How were you a responsible partner
and learner while doing this activity?**

**Q. How were you considerate of each
other's "think" time?**

**Q. How did you share your solutions?
Do you think you did it in a way that
was fair to both of you? Why?**

Have pairs fasten their Number Cards
together with a paper clip and place them
in their group folder.

To help students continue to develop
informal computation and estimation
strategies, have them explore the Extensions before going on to the next lesson.

•• ••

•• ••

**For the
Next Day**

Extensions

- Display other pairs' sets of Number Cards and discuss questions
  similar to those in the lesson.

- Begin the ongoing "Number Card Activity" described in the
  Overview, p. 123.

First and Last Names 2

Students practice adding numbers together using sets of Number Cards from Lesson 3. They also explain and record each other's strategies.

Mathematical Emphasis

In this lesson, students

- Use a variety of computational strategies.
- Record each other's strategies.

Students add to their understanding that

- Operations can be carried out in a variety of ways to arrive at an accurate solution.
- Numbers can be composed and decomposed.

Social Emphasis

In this lesson, students

- Help each other when asked.
- Explain their thinking.
- Listen to each other.
- Ask questions about the thinking of others.
- Check for agreement.

Students continue to

- Develop group skills.
- Analyze why it is important to be fair, caring, and responsible.
- Analyze the effect of behavior on others and on the group work.

Teacher Materials

- Pocket chart

Student Materials

Each pair needs

- Access to group folder (containing Number Cards)
- Access to counters and Hundred Chart (see Unit 1, Lesson 3)
- Paper and a pencil

Extension Materials

Each pair needs

- Access to group folder (containing Number Cards)
- Paper and a pencil

Group Size: 2

Have students work with the same partner as in Lesson 3.

Have pairs discuss what they did in the previous lesson, "First and Last Names 1." Ask questions such as:

Q. What did you do with the Number Cards?

Q. What did you do in the previous lesson that helped you work well with your partner? How did it help you?

Explain that pairs will exchange their set of number cards with the other pair in their group. Pairs will use the new set of Number Cards to solve problems and record strategies.

Use a pair's set of cards to model the activity with a student as your partner:

1. Place the cards in a stack face down, and ask your partner to turn over the top two cards in the stack. For example:

Having one partner record while the other partner solves the problem, then reversing roles, gives both partners experience communicating their thinking so another person can understand, and experience listening to a strategy and recording it accurately. Remind students that it is important that both partners agree on each solution.

2. Ask your partner to be the problem solver and to add the two numbers and explain his or her solution and strategy.

3. Act as the recorder, and record the two numbers and your partner's solution and strategy where all can see. For example:

12   19

The total is 31. I took 1 from 12 and added it to 19 to make 20. Then I added the 11 to 20 and got 31.

Model this activity several times.

4. Check to make sure you both agree on the answer, then reverse roles and repeat the activity.

Social Emphasis

Analyze why it is important to be fair, caring, and responsible.

Before students begin to work, facilitate a discussion about how partners might work together. Ask questions such as:

Q. **How can you help your partner understand your strategy? Why is this important?**

Q. **How can you make sure you are listening to what your partner is saying? If you don't understand your partner, what can you say to get more information without hurting your partner's feelings? Why is this important?**

Q. **If your partner needs help writing your strategy, how can you give help without doing the writing yourself?**

Q. **Why is it important that you both agree on the solution?**

Have pairs remove their set of Number Cards from their group folder and exchange with the other pair in their group. Ask pairs to place the cards in a stack, decide who will be the problem solver and recorder for the first problem, and then begin the activity.

•• ••

•• ••

As you observe pairs, ask yourself questions such as:

Q. What strategies are students using to solve the problem? Are they recognizing combinations of numbers that can be added easily (for example, addends that equal ten or a multiple of ten)?

Q. How are pairs working together? How are they showing respect for each other's thinking time? Have they grown in their ability to listen to each other?

Observe pairs and ask questions such as:

Q. **How did you decide who would be the problem solver and who would be the recorder?**

Q. **What two numbers are you adding together? Do you think the total will be more or less than [40]? How do you know?**

Q. **How are you making sure your partner understands what you are saying? How are you making sure you are listening to your partner?**

•• In pairs, students

1. Decide which partner will be the problem solver and which partner will be the recorder for the first problem.

2. Depending on their role, either find the sum of the numbers on the top two cards and explain their strategy, or record the numbers, the sum, and the strategy.

3. Check for agreement, correct any errors, and then reverse roles and repeat the activity.

Mathematical Emphasis

Operations can be carried out in a variety of ways to arrive at an accurate solution.

Social Emphasis

Analyze the effect of behavior on others and on the group work.

Have several pairs choose one of the problems they solved to share with the class. Ask questions such as:

Q. **What questions would you like to ask this pair about this strategy?**

Q. **Who used a similar strategy? Explain. Who used a different strategy? Explain.**

First in pairs, then as a class, have students reflect on how they worked with their partner. Discuss questions such as:

Q. **What did you like about working together?**

Q. **What were some ways you helped your partner when he or she was the problem solver? Recorder? How did that help your work together?**

Have pairs fasten their set of Number Cards together with a paper clip and place them into their group folder.

To help students continue to develop informal computational strategies, have pairs explore the Extensions before going on to the next lesson.

Extensions

For the Next Day

- Have pairs repeat the activity using three Number Cards at a time, rather than two.

- Continue the ongoing "Number Card Activity" described in the Overview, p. 123.

Tea Party!

Students compare quantities and explore informal subtraction strategies using their Number Cards and the "Tea Party" strategy.

Mathematical Emphasis

In this lesson, students

- Compare quantities to find the difference.
- Estimate differences.
- Use mental computation.

Students add to their understanding that

- Operations can be carried out in a variety of ways to arrive at an accurate solution.
- Making a reasonable estimate requires gathering and using information.

Social Emphasis

In this lesson, students

- Explain their thinking.
- Move responsibly around the room.

Students continue to

- Develop group skills.
- Take responsibility for learning and behavior.

Group Size: 2

Student Materials

Each pair needs

- Access to group folder (containing Number Cards)

Extension Materials

Each student needs

- Access to group folder (containing Number Cards)

■ In this lesson, students use a cooperative strategy called "Tea Party" (see p. xii). If students have not used the "Tea Party" strategy, have them practice it prior to this lesson.

Notes	Teacher	Students

Introduce the lesson by having students recall how they added the numbers on the cards in the previous lessons. Explain that pairs will participate in a class "Tea Party" in which they will compare the numbers on two cards to find the difference between them.

Randomly select a Number Card from a pair's set of cards. Have each pair also select one card from their group folder. Hold up your number and compare it to another pair's number. As a class, discuss questions such as:

Q. What can you say about our two numbers?

For example, students' explanations for comparing 25 and 11 might be:

■ "I counted on from 11 to 25 and found out that 25 is 14 more than 11."

■ "I doubled 11 and got 22. Then I added 3 more to 22 to make 25. 11 and 3 is 14, so the difference is 14."

Q. What is the difference between these two numbers? How did you figure it out? Did someone do it in a different way?

Repeat the activity several times by comparing other pairs' Number Cards to your card.

Review the "Tea Party" strategy. Have students suggest and model responsible ways to move around the room and to include everyone in the discussion during the "Tea Party."

If students have difficulty determining differences using mental computation, consider having pairs sit down together at a table at each "Tea Party" stop and providing access to Hundred Charts, counters, and paper and pencil at each table.

Have each pair take their Number Card and move around the room. Call "Tea Party," and have pairs stop and form a group of four with another pair. Have groups of four discuss their Number Cards.

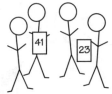

Notes	Teacher	Students

Teacher

At each "Tea Party" stop, discuss one or two of the following questions:

Q. **What can you tell the class about the numbers on your cards?**

Q. **Does any group have numbers with a difference close to [10]? How do you know?**

Q. **What is the difference between your two numbers? How do you know? What is another strategy a group used?**

Q. **How are you making sure to listen to each other's ideas? Why is this a fair way?**

Repeat the "Tea Party" activity several times.

Have pairs return to their seats. Help students reflect on the lesson by asking questions such as:

Q. **What are some strategies you used to find the difference between two numbers?**

Q. **What did you find interesting about the "Tea Party"? Why?**

Q. **How did you move around the room in a responsible way?**

Q. **How did you make sure that you were participating in the discussion at each "Tea Party" stop?**

Ask pairs to fasten their Number Cards together with a paper clip and place them into their group folder.

To help students continue to develop informal subtraction strategies, have them explore the Extensions before going on to Lesson 6.

Notes

Mathematical Emphasis
Operations can be carried out in a variety of ways to arrive at an accurate solution.

Social Emphasis
Take responsibility for learning and behavior.

**For the
Next Day**

■ Ask each student to choose a Number Card from his or her group folder. Have a "Tea Party" with individual students moving around the room and joining another student to form a pair at each "Tea Party" stop.

At each "Tea Party" stop, ask questions similar to the ones in the lesson.

■ Have pairs use their set of Number Cards to estimate the difference between two numbers by asking questions such as:

Q. Do you have any two numbers that have a difference of around [25]? How do you know?

Repeat the activity several times using differences of 5, 10, 15, and 20.

What's the Difference?

Students draw two Number Cards, individually find the difference between the two numbers, agree on the solution with their partner, and record one of their strategies.

Mathematical Emphasis

In this lesson, students

- Compare quantities to find the difference.
- Write statements about differences.
- Estimate differences.

Students add to their understanding that

- Operations can be carried out in a variety of ways to arrive at an accurate solution.
- Making a reasonable estimate requires gathering and using information.

Social Emphasis

In this lesson, students

- Give each other time to solve problems individually.
- Explain their thinking.
- Share the work.
- Reach agreement.

Students continue to

- Develop group skills.
- Analyze why it is important to be fair, caring, and responsible.

Group Size: 2

Teacher Materials

- Paper lunch bag containing Number Cards for each pair (see Before the Lesson)

Student Materials

Each pair needs

- Access to counters and Hundred Chart (see Unit 1, Lesson 3)
- Paper and a pencil
- Access to group folder

Extension Materials

Each pair needs

- Paper lunch bag with Number Cards (from the lesson)
- Access to counters and Hundred Chart
- Paper and a pencil

- Collect pairs' Number Cards from their group folders and randomly distribute the cards into paper lunch bags. You will need one bag with approximately 6–8 cards for each pair.

Notes	Teacher	Students

Facilitate a discussion about how partners have worked together by asking questions such as:

•• ••

•• ••

Social Emphasis
Relate the values of fairness, caring, and responsibility to behavior.

Q. How have you been respectful of your partners' thinking and ideas? Why is this important?

Q. Why is it important to give others and yourself "think" time before starting to discuss your thinking?

Q. What problems have you had working together? How might these problems be solved in a fair way?

Explain that each pair will get a bag with some Number Cards. Pairs will take two cards from the bag, compare the numbers on the cards, and individually find the difference between the two numbers. Partners will share their strategies, agree on the solution, and record one of their strategies on a sheet of paper.

To model the activity, have a student act as your partner and select two Number Cards from a bag. Record the two numbers where all can see. For example:

> 35   17

Notes	**Teacher**	**Students**

Notes

To find the difference between two numbers, students might mentally count on or take away, use counters, or use a paper and pencil strategy. If students use a standard subtraction algorithm, encourage them to verify their answer using another method as well.

Mathematical Emphasis

Operations can be carried out in a variety of ways to arrive at an accurate solution.

Teacher

Individually find the difference between the two numbers, discuss your strategies with each other, agree on the solution, and choose one of your strategies to record. Then model recording the strategy.

> 35   17
>
> • 17 is 18 less than 35. I know this because 17 and 17 is 34. One more makes 35. So 17 and 18 is 35.

Model the activity as many times as seems appropriate.

Distribute a paper bag with Number Cards to each pair. Ask pairs to take two cards from the bag, record the numbers, set the cards aside, and individually find the difference between the two numbers. Explain that partners will then share their strategies with each other, agree on the solution, record one of their strategies, and repeat the activity with two new Number Cards.

Students

•• ••

•• ••

As you observe pairs, ask yourself questions such as:

Q. What strategies are students using to find the differences?

Q. How are partners being respectful of each other's "think" time?

Q. How clearly are students explaining their thinking to each other?

Observe pairs and ask questions such as:

Q. How are you making sure to give each other time to solve the problem? Does this seem to be working? Why? Why not? What else can you try?

Q. How did your partner solve this problem? Did you both solve it in the same way?

Q. How are you agreeing on which strategies to record? How is this fair?

Q. How do you know that [15] is [13] less than [28]? Do you both agree? If not, what can you do to come to agreement?

••   In pairs, students

1. Draw two Number Cards from the paper bag, record the numbers, and set the cards aside.

2. Individually find the difference between the two numbers.

3. Discuss their strategies with each other, agree on the solution, and record one of their strategies.

4. Repeat the activity with two new cards.

•• ••

•• ••

Have several pairs share one of their solutions with the class. Discuss questions such as:

Students might say:

- "I counted up from the smaller number to the larger number."
- "My partner used a Hundred Chart and counted backward by tens and ones from the larger number to the smaller number."
- "My partner counted out the larger number in cubes, took the smaller number away and counted how many cubes were left."

Q. What was a strategy you or your partner used to find the difference?

Q. Did anyone find two numbers with a difference around [20]? What were your two numbers? What might be two other numbers that would have a difference around [20]? Explain.

Q. [Marissa] and [Ian] drew [47] and [19]. Without computing the answer exactly, is the difference more or less than [20]? How do you know?

Help students reflect on how they were respectful and considerate of each other's thinking during the lesson. If appropriate, share some of your observations of the positive interactions and problems you noted as pairs worked.

Have pairs put their papers into their group folder. Collect the paper bags with the Number Cards for use in Extensions.

Extensions

For the Next Day

- Explain that pairs will use two numbers drawn from a paper bag to write addition and subtraction stories. Model the activity by taking two Number Cards from a bag and using the numbers to write addition and subtraction stories with the class. For example:

17　41

My brother is 17 years old. My uncle is 41. My uncle is 24 years older than my brother.

There are 17 chocolate chip cookies in this jar. In the other jar there are 41 peanut butter cookies. There are 58 cookies.

Have pairs draw two Number Cards from the paper bag and use the numbers to write addition and subtraction stories. Have pairs share their stories with the class.

Stupendous Students

Students reflect on, discuss, and write about their mathematical ideas and their work together during the unit.

DAYS AHEAD
2
TRANSITION

Transition Emphasis

In this lesson, students

- Reflect on their mathematical ideas and work from the unit.
- Write about their work.
- Thank each other.

Students add to their understanding that

- Numbers can be used to describe quantities.

Social Emphasis

In this lesson, students

- Reflect on how they worked together.
- Contribute ideas to a class book.

Students continue to

- Develop group skills.
- Be fair and caring when relating to others.

Group Size: 4

Teacher Materials

- 12″ × 18″ sheet of drawing paper for each student and for yourself (see Before the Lesson)
- "Number of Letters in Our First Names" graph (from Lesson 2)

Student Materials

Each group of four needs

- Access to a dictionary (see Before the Lesson)
- Group folder

Each student needs

- Their self-portrait page (see Before the Lesson)

Extension Materials

- Class book (from the lesson)

I wrote, "I liked finding out about our names and making the First Names graph for our group. And I liked how my partner helped me think about the numbers".

■ For demonstration purposes, draw a self-portrait on the left-hand side of a 12″× 18″ sheet of drawing paper. Below your self portrait, write your first name preceded by a descriptive word that starts with the same letter or sound. For example:

■ Use a second sheet of 12″× 18″ drawing paper to make a cover for a class book entitled, "Stupendous Students." For example:

■ One day before the lesson, show the cover to the students, read and discuss the title, "Stupendous Students," and explain that each student will contribute a page to this class book. Model the activity by showing students your self-portrait page and reading your descriptive name. Share other examples of descriptive names that begin with a word having the same letter or sound as the first name (for example, Peppy Pablo, Happy Harry, and Nifty Nora).

Ask groups to work together to come up with a similar descriptive name for each group member. You may want to have dictionaries available for each group. Using your self-portrait page as a model, explain that after all group members have a name, each student will write his or her name on the bottom of a 12″ × 18″ sheet of drawing paper, then draw a self-portrait on the left side of the drawing paper, leaving the right side blank.

After students have completed their self-portrait pages, have students share their pages first with their group, then with the class.

Collect and save the self-portrait pages.

| **Notes** | **Teacher** | **Students** |

Post the "Number of Letters in Our First Names" graph from Lesson 2.

Introduce the lesson by explaining that students will review and discuss the work in their group folder, then write statements about their experiences in this unit on their self-portrait pages. Have students, first in groups, then as a class, discuss questions such as:

:: ::
:: ::
:: ::
:: ::

Q. **What are some of the activities you participated in during this unit? What is something you really liked about one of the activities?**

Q. **What did we find out about the letters in our names? How did we find out?**

Mathematical Emphasis
Numbers can be used to describe quantities.

Q. **How did you use numbers in these lessons? What other mathematics did we explore?**

Q. **What is one thing you can now do mathematically that you couldn't do before?**

Q. **What did you learn about adding and subtracting numbers? When do you add and subtract numbers outside of school?**

Q. **What are some ways you and your group or partner helped each other learn?**

Q. **What did you learn about solving problems when working with others? How did this help you?**

Modeling your thinking aloud helps students to reflect on their own learning.

Display your self-portrait page, and model the activity by thinking aloud and recording on the page your thoughts about the unit's mathematics and how the class worked together during the unit. For example:

I liked the Tea Party because we compared numbers and found the differences. We talked with several different pairs and shared our thinking.

Shimmering Sharon

Notes	Teacher	Students

Ask groups to discuss the work in their folders, individually write some statements about their experiences in the blank space on their self-portrait pages, and share their self-portrait pages with their group.

⬛⬛ ⬛⬛
⬛⬛ ⬛⬛

As you observe students, note any ideas in students' written statements that you might want to discuss when the class reflects on the unit. Also note ways students have changed in their ability to listen to each other and take responsibility for their own learning.

Observe students and ask questions such as:

Q. **How did you use numbers in this lesson?**

Q. (Refer to a student's written statement.) **What else might you tell someone about this activity?**

Q. **How did listening to others help you learn?**

Q. **What might you do differently next time?**

⬛⬛   In groups, students
⬛⬛

1. Discuss the work in their group folder.

2. Individually decide on and write some statements about their work on their self-portrait page.

3. Share their self-portrait page with their group.

Have several groups share their self-portrait pages with the class. Facilitate a class discussion by asking questions such as:

Q. **What was something that surprised you when you shared your pages together?**

Q. **In what ways were your ideas similar? Different?**

Help students reflect on their work together by asking questions such as:

Social Emphasis
Be fair and caring when relating to others.

Q. **During the lesson, how did people in your group share the work fairly and show each other they cared about others' ideas?**

Q. **Why is it important to be respectful of each other's "think" time?**

Q. **What might you do differently next time you work with others?**

⬛⬛ ⬛⬛
⬛⬛ ⬛⬛

Notes	**Teacher**	**Students**
	You may want to share your observations about how students and the class worked together during the unit. Give group members an opportunity to thank each other. Collect the self-portrait pages and bind them into a class book titled "Stupendous Students" for use in Extensions For the Next Day.	

Extensions

For Students That Finish Early

- Have students brainstorm and list situations outside of school in which they would need to add or subtract. Provide time for students to share their lists with others in their group or with the class.

For the Next Day

- Read the class book "Stupendous Students" to the class. Have the book available in the class library for students to read on their own.

- Continue with the ongoing "Number Cards Activity" described in the Overview, p. 123.

Additional Reading

Mathematics Education

California State Department of Education. *Mathematics Framework for California Public Schools, Kindergarten Through Grade Twelve.* Sacramento, CA: California State Department of Education, 1992.

———. *Mathematics Model Curriculum Guide, Kindergarten Through Grade Eight.* Sacramento, CA: California State Department of Education, 1987.

Ginsberg, Herbert P. *The Development of Mathematical Thinking.* New York: Academic Press, 1983.

Kamii, Constance. *Number in Preschool and Kindergarten.* Washington, DC: National Association for the Education of Young Children (NAEYC), 1982.

———. *Young Children Reinvent Arithmetic.* New York: Teachers College Press, 1985.

———. *Young Children Continue to Reinvent Arithmetic,* 2nd Grade. New York: Teachers College Press, 1989.

Kamii, Constance, and Barbara A. Lewis. "Research into Practice: Constructive Learning and Teaching." *Arithmetic Teacher,* 38 (1990), pp. 34–35.

Labinowicz, Ed. *The Piaget Primer.* Reading, MA: Addison-Wesley Publishing Company, 1980.

———. *Learning from Children: New Beginnings for Teaching Numerical Thinking.* Menlo Park, CA: Addison-Wesley Publishing Company, 1985.

Mathematical Sciences Education Board. *On the Shoulders of Giants.* National Research Council, Washington, DC: National Academy Press, 1990.

National Council of Teachers of Mathematics. *Communication in Mathematics, K–12 and Beyond.* 1996 Yearbook. Reston, VA: National Council of Teachers of Mathematics, 1996.

———. *Connecting Mathematics Across the Curriculum.* 1995 Yearbook. Reston, VA: National Council of Teachers of Mathematics, 1995.

———. *Developing Computational Skills.* 1978 Yearbook. Reston, VA: National Council of Teachers of Mathematics, 1978.

———. *Estimation and Mental Computation.* 1986 Yearbook. Reston, VA: National Council of Teachers of Mathematics, 1986.

———. *The Ideas of Algebra, K Through 12.* 1988 Yearbook. Reston, VA: National Council of Teachers of Mathematics, 1988.

———. *Arithmetic Teacher,* 36 (1989). Special focus issue on number sense.

———. *Curriculum and Evaluation Standards for School Mathematics.* Reston, VA: National Council of Teachers of Mathematics, 1989.

———. *Curriculum and Evaluation Standards for School Mathematics Addenda Series, Grades K Through 6.* Reston, VA: National Council of Teachers of Mathematics, 1991.

———. *Curriculum and Evaluation Standards for School Mathematics Addenda Series, Grades 5 Through 8.* Reston, VA: National Council of Teachers of Mathematics, 1991.

———. *Multicultural and Gender Equity in the Mathematics Classroom.* 1997 Yearbook. Reston, VA: National Council of Teachers of Mathematics, 1997.

———. *New Directions for Elementary School Mathematics.* 1989 Yearbook. Reston, VA: National Council of Teachers of Mathematics, 1989.

———. *Professional Standards for Teaching Mathematics.* Reston, VA: National Council of Teachers of Mathematics, 1991.

———. *Teaching and Learning Mathematics in the 1990s.* 1990 Yearbook. Reston, VA: National Council of Teachers of Mathematics, 1990.

National Research Council. *Everybody Counts: A Report to the Nation on the Future of Mathematics Education.* Washington, DC: National Academy Press, 1989.

———. *Reshaping School Mathematics: A Philosophy and Framework for Curriculum.* Washington, DC: National Academy Press, 1990.

Sowder, Judith T., and Bonnie P. Schappelle, eds. *Establishing Foundations for Research on Number Sense and Related Topics: Report of a Conference.* San Diego, CA: Center for Research in Mathematics and Science Education, 1989.

Stenmark, Jean K. (ed). *Mathematics Assessment: Myths, Models, Good Questions, and Practical Suggestions.* Reston, VA: National Council of Teachers of Mathematics, 1991.

———. *Assessment Alternatives in Mathematics: An Overview of Assessment Techniques That Promote Learning.* Berkeley, CA: Lawrence Hall of Science, University of California, 1989.

Cooperative Learning and Moral Development

Artzt, Alice F., and Claire M. Newman. *How to Use Cooperative Learning in the Mathematics Class.* Reston, VA: National Council of Teachers of Mathematics, 1990.

Brandt, Ron (ed). *Cooperative Learning.* Educational Leadership, 1989–90, 47.

Brubacher, Mark, Ryder Payne, and Kemp Rickett. *Perspectives on Small Group Learning, Theory, and Practice.* New York: Rubicon Publishing Inc., 1990.

Cohen, Elizabeth G. *Designing Groupwork: Strategies for the Heterogenous Classroom.* New York, NY: Teachers College Press, 1986.

Dalton, Joan and Marilyn Watson. *Among Friends: Classrooms Where Caring and Learning Prevail.* Oakland, CA: Developmental Studies Center, 1997.

Davidson, Neil, ed. *Cooperative Learning in Mathematics: A Handbook for Teachers.* Menlo Park, CA: Addison-Wesley Publishing Co., 1990.

Developmental Studies Center. *Blueprints for a Collaborative Classroom.* Oakland, CA: Developmental Studies Center, 1997.

———. *Ways We Want Our Class to Be: Class Meetings that Build Commitment to Kindness and Learning.* Oakland, CA: Developmental Studies Center, 1997.

Johnson, David. W., et al. *Circles of Learning: Cooperation in the Classroom.* Alexandria, VA: Association for Supervision and Curriculum Development, 1986.

Kohlberg, Lawrence. "Moral Stages and Moralization: The Cognitive Developmental Approach." In *Moral Development and Behavior,* T. Lickona, ed. New York: Holt, Rinehart and Winston, 1976.

———. *The Psychology of Moral Development.* New York: Harper and Row, 1984.

Kohn, Alfie. "The ABC's of Caring." *Teacher,* 1 (1990), 52–58.

———. "Teaching Children to Care." *Phi Delta Kappan,* 72 (1991), pp. 496–506.

Lickona, Thomas. *Raising Good Children.* New York: Bantam Books, 1983.

Reid, Jo-Anne, Peter Forrestal, and Jonathan Cook. *Small Group Learning in the Classroom.* Scarborough, West Australia: Chalkface Press, 1989.

Schmuck, Richard A., and Patricia A. Schmuck. *Group Processes in the Classroom.* Dubuque, IA: Wm. C. Brown, Company, 1983.

Schniedewind, Nancy. *Cooperative Learning, Cooperative Lives.* Dubuque, IA: Wm. C. Brown, Company, 1983.

Sharan, Shlomo. *Cooperative Learning, Theory, and Research.* New York: Praeger, 1990.

Teacher Resource Books

Baker, Ann, and Johnny Baker. *Mathematics in Process.* Portsmouth, NH: Heinemann Educational Books, Inc., 1990.

———. *Maths in the Mind.* Portsmouth, NH: Heinemann Educational Books, Inc., 1991.

Barata-Lorton, Mary. *Mathematics Their Way.* Menlo Park, CA: Addison-Wesley Publishing Company, 1976.

Barnett, Carne. *Teaching Kids Math.* Englewood Cliffs, NJ: Prentice Hall, Inc., 1982.

Burns, Marilyn. *About Teaching Mathematics, A K Through 8 Resource.* White Plains, NY: Cuisenaire Company of America, 1992.

———. *A Collection of Math Lessons from Grades 3 Through 6.* White Plains, NY: Cuisenaire Company of America, 1987.

———. *Math by All Means, Multiplication: Grade 3.* White Plains, NY: Cuisenaire Company of America, 1991.

Burns, Marilyn and Cathy McLaughlin. *A Collection of Math Lessons from Grades 6 Through 8.* White Plains, NY: Cuisenaire Company of America, 1990.

Burns, Marilyn, and Bonnie Tank. *A Collection of Math Lessons from Grades 1 Through 3.* White Plains, NY: Cuisenaire Company of America, 1988.

Collis, Mark, and Joan Dalton. *Becoming Responsible Learners: Strategies for Positive Classroom Management.* Portsmouth, NH: Heinemann Educational Books, Inc., 1990

Dalton, Joan. *Adventures in Thinking: Creative Thinking and Cooperative Talk in Small Groups.* South Melbourne, Australia: Thomas Nelson Australia, 1990.

Elementary Grades Task Force. *It's Elementary!* Sacramento, CA: California Department of Education, 1992.

EQUALS. *Get It Together: Math Problems for Groups, Grades 4 Through 12.* Berkeley, CA: Lawrence Hall of Science, University of California, 1989.

EQUALS, Alice Kaseberg, Nancy Kreinberg, and Diane Downie. *Use EQUALS to Promote the Participation of Women in Mathematics.* Berkeley, CA: Regents of the University of California, 1980.

Gibbs, Jeanne, and Andre Allen. *Tribes: A Process for Peer Involvement.* Santa Rosa, CA: Center Source Publications, 1987.

Graves, Ted, and Nan Graves. *A Part to Play: Tips, Techniques and Tools for Learning Cooperatively.* Victoria, Australia: Latitude Publications, 1990.

Hill, Susan, and Ted Hill. *The Collaborative Classroom.* Portsmouth, NH: Heinemann Educational Books, Inc., 1990.

Kagan, Spencer. *Cooperative Learning.* San Juan Capistrano, CA: Resources of Teachers, 1992.

Lappan, Glenda, William Fitzgerald, Elizabeth Phillips, Janet Shroyer, and Mary Jean Winter. *Middle Grades Mathematics Project.* Menlo Park, CA: Addison-Wesley Publishing Company, 1986. A series of five books for grades 6 through 9.

Meyer, Carol and Tom Salee. *Make It Simpler: A Practical Guide to Problem Solving.* Menlo Park, CA: Addison-Wesley Publishing Company, 1983.

Morman, Chuck, and Dee Dishon. *Our Classroom: We Can Learn Together.* Portage, MI: The Institute for Personal Power, 1983.

Rhodes, Jacqueline, and Margaret E. McCabe. *The Nurturing Classroom.* Willits, CA: ITA Publications, 1988.

Richardson, Kathy. *Developing Number Concepts Using Unifix Cubes.* Menlo Park, CA: Addison-Wesley Publishing Company, 1984.

Russell, Susan Jo, Rebecca Corwin, and Susan Friel. *Used Numbers: Real Data in the Classroom.* Palo Alto, CA: Dale Seymour Publications, 1990. A series of six books for grades K through 6.

Stenmark, Jean, K., Virginia Thompson, and Ruth Cossey. *Family Math.* Berkeley, CA: Lawrence Hall of Science, University of California, 1986.

Whitin, David J., Heidi Mills, and Timothy O'Keefe. *Living and Learning Mathematics.* Portsmouth, NH: Heinemann Educational Books, Inc., 1990.

Wilson, Jeni, and Peter Egeberg. *Co-operative Challenges and Student Investigations.* South Melbourne, Australia: Thomas Nelson Australia, 1990.